Knight's Cross Profiles Volume 2

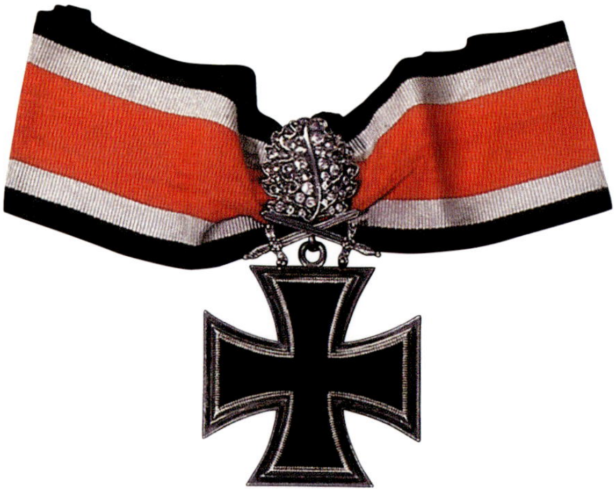

Knight's Cross Profiles

Volume 2

Gerhard Türke • Heinrich "Heinz" Bär
Arnold Huebner • Joachim Müncheberg

Ralf Schumann

Schiffer Military History
Atglen, PA

Book translation by David Johnston
Book Design by John P. Cheek.

Copyright © 2013 by Ralf Schumann.
Library of Congress Control Number: 2012931291

All rights reserved. No part of this work may be reproduced or used in any forms or by any means – graphic, electronic or mechanical, including photocopying or information storage and retrieval systems – without written permission from the copyright holder.

This book is a combination of works originally published in German under the series title *Ritterkreuzträger* by Flugzeug Publikations GmbH

Printed in China.
ISBN: 978-0-7643-4369-8

We are interested in hearing from authors with book ideas on related topics.

Published by Schiffer Publishing Ltd. 4880 Lower Valley Road Atglen, PA 19310 Phone: (610) 593-1777 FAX: (610) 593-2002 E-mail: Info@schifferbooks.com. Visit our web site at: www.schifferbooks.com Please write for a free catalog. This book may be purchased from the publisher. Try your bookstore first.	In Europe, Schiffer books are distributed by: Bushwood Books 6 Marksbury Avenue Kew Gardens Surrey TW9 4JF, England Phone: 44 (0) 20 8392-8585 FAX: 44 (0) 20 8392-9876 E-mail: Info@bushwoodbooks.co.uk. Visit our website at: www.bushwoodbooks.co.uk Try your bookstore first.

Gerhard Türke

A Knight's Cross Winner from the Stalingrad Pocket

BY RALF SCHUMANN

Foreword

In the history of WWII, the battle for the city of Stalingrad holds a chapter of its own. Thousands of Russian and German soldiers lost their lives there in a senseless struggle. Many of those who fought there, believing in the justness of their cause, remain nameless. Only a few escaped the inferno.

One of them was Gerhard Türke, at the time an *Oberleutnant* der Reserve, who took part in the fighting as a member of the 3rd Motorized Infantry Division and won the Knight's Cross for his personal bravery in the battle for the city on the Volga. He was wounded and flown out of the city, thus avoiding the fate of many who were taken prisoner.

This volume will not only describe his military career, but also the history of an entire division, with all its highs and lows. Gerhard Türke, who served in the 3rd Motorized Infantry Division – later reformed as the 3rd Panzer Grenadier Division – from the time he joined the army as a volunteer in 1936 until he was captured in April 1945, took part in the division's campaigns on every front and remains closely linked to it. Whether in Poland and France, the expanses of Russia, or action in Italy against the Allied invasion forces, or finally on German soil, he experienced its martyrdom.

Ralf Schumann

Decorations:

October 1939	Iron Cross, Second Class
10 July 1940	Commemorative Medal of the Return of the Memel District
21 January 1941	Iron Cross, First Class
21 January 1941	Infantry Assault Badge in Silver
21 January 1941	Wound Badge in Black
July 1942	Medal for the Winter Campaign in Russia 1941-42
17 December 1942	Knight's Cross of the Iron Cross
13 June 1944	Close Combat Bar in Silver
22 December 1944	German Cross in Gold

Promotions:

20 April 1939	Leutnant der Reserve
1 February 1942	Oberleutnant der Reserve
1 December 1942	Hauptmann der Reserve
1 November 1944	Major (transferred to the army's active officer corps)

Campaigns:

1938	Occupation of the Memel District
1939	Polish Campaign
1940	Western Campaign
1941-42	Russian Campaign
1942	Battle of Stalingrad
1943-44	Italy
1944-45	Battle of the Reich

Gerhard Türke was promoted to Major on 1 November 1944. The members of his staff made this card to congratulate their commanding officer. The caption reads: "Congratulations to the marauder from the happy battalion."

Education and Training

Gerhard Türke was born 1 May 1914 in Heinsersdorf, in the Lebus District of Brandenburg, the son of a carpenter.

After attending the local village school and the middle school in Müncheberg, he went to the vocational school in Fürstenwalde/Spree. After graduation, he immediately volunteered for the Labor Service and completed his tour in Gross-Strehlitz (Upper Silesia), soon becoming a foreman and troop leader. From 1934 to 1936 he attended teacher's college in Frankfurt an der Oder.

On 1 April 1936 he was given a teaching position in Herzendorf, near Guben. By then, however, Germany had regained military sovereignty, and the expansion of the *Wehrmacht* was under way.

On 1 July 1936 Türke joined Infantry Regiment 29 as a volunteer. The regiment was part of the 3rd Brandenburg Infantry Division, which had emerged from *Reichswehr* Division No. 3. Its garrisons were in East Brandenburg, and 90 percent of its troops came from Mark Brandenburg. In March 1939, Türke took part in the entry into the Memel District (Memelland). Later, on 10 July 1940, he was awarded the so-called Memelland Medal.

Türke was promoted to *Oberleutnant der Reserve* (d.R.) on 20 April 1939.

Gerhard Türke joined the *Wehrmacht* on 1 July 1936.

Proud soldier in Infantry Regiment 29.

Gefreiter Türke (right) with comrades during a field exercise.

Türke was promoted to *Leutnant* on 20 April 1939.

Outbreak of WWII

Türke's regiment took part in the Polish Campaign under the command of *Oberst* Fritz-Hubert Gräser, who had been named regimental commander on 1 September 1939. Under his command the regiment broke through the chain of lakes west of Crone. It crossed the Vistula near Topolno-Grabowko and marched towards Modlin. With the division it secured the Bzura pocket, and in the Woclawek-Wyscogrod area the advance by neighboring army units. This was followed by an attack on both sides of Plock and subsequent advance towards Gostynin before the division turned towards Lowicz.

In mid-September Gerhard Türke, who led a platoon in the 2nd Company of Infantry Regiment 29, succeeded in freeing 300 German soldiers from the Protestant church in Ilow. The men had been captured by the Poles and were waiting transport out. The campaign ended in late September, and Gerhard Türke was decorated with the Iron Cross, Second Class.

From 4 November 1939 to 9 May 1940, the division was stationed in the Schnee Eifel to guard the frontier west of the Siegfried Line (*Westwall*). After spending half a year in the Eifel, on 10 May 1940 Gerhard Türke and his comrades found themselves taking part in the German offensive in the west. The division marched 140 kilometers in four days. After company commander *Hauptmann* Pauck was killed, *Leutnant* Türke took over as acting commander.

Route march – second from the left is *Leutnant* Gerhard Türke.

In formation for roll call.

Meal break in the Westwall during the frontier defense period in early 1940.

The way "his" men liked him.

Shortly before the start of the Western Campaign in 1940.

Action on the Western Front

The record of Türke's actions reads like a summary of events from those days: guarding Germany's western frontier; advance through Luxembourg and breaching the south-Belgian fortifications in the Ardennes and preliminary fighting at the Semois River; fighting for the Belgian frontier fortifications in the Bastogne—St. Hubertz—Libramonth area; breakthrough battle at Sedan and Charville; breakthrough at Nounzonville; pursuit of the enemy from the Meuse to the Oise and the Aisne; combat near Asfeld-la-Ville and Balham; defensive fighting near La Fère, on the Chemin-des-Dames, and at the Aisne River; piercing of the French front on the Aisne River and astride Asfeld-la-Ville; pursuit of the enemy through Champagne and across the Rhine-Marne Canal to the Swiss border; fighting for the Rhine-Marne Canal and the Marne fortifications west of St. Dizier; fighting pursuit to capture the Langres Plateau; and pursuit on both sides of the Côte d'Or and the securing of the demarcation line.

Commander *Oberst* Gräser was awarded the Knight's Cross on 19 July 1940 for successfully forcing a crossing of the Aisne near Asfeld.

Leutnant Türke was awarded the Iron Cross, First Class on 21 January 1941. He also received the Infantry Assault Badge in Silver and the Wound Badge in Black. And so, for Gerhard Türke the campaign in the west came to an end. This was followed by the reorganization of the 3rd Infantry Division into a motorized division in the garrisons and at Training Camp Wandern. IR 50 left the division and became part of the 111th ID.

After the advance through Belgium.

At the firing range in Guben, 1941.

***General der Panzertruppe* Fritz-Hubert Gräser. He commanded Infantry Regiment 29 in France in 1940 and the newly-formed 3rd Panzer Grenadier Division in Italy in 1944.**

Im Namen des Führers und Obersten Befehlshabers der Wehrmacht

verleihe ich

dem

Leutnant

Gerhard T ü r k e

2./J.R.(mot)29

das

Eiserne Kreuz 1. Klasse.

................O.U........,den..21.Januar...1941

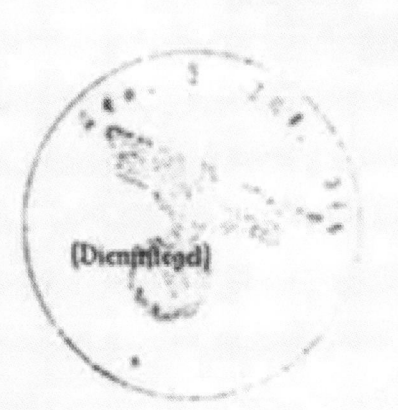

(Dienstsiegel)

Generalleutnant und Kommandeur
der 3.Infanteriedivision (mot)
(Dienstgrad und Dienststellung)

War against the Soviet Union

When the Eastern Campaign began in 1941, Türke experienced the rapid advance into the Soviet Union. The division was part of LVI Motorized Army Corps under *Generalleutnant* Erwin von Manstein, born von Lewinski (1887-1973, Knight's Cross on 19 July 1940 as *General der Infanterie* and commanding general of the XXXVIII Army Corps, 209th Oak Leaves on 14 March 1943 and 59th Swords on 30 March 1944 as *Generalfeldmarschall,* and Commander-in-Chief of Army Group South), which was part of Army Group North. Its objective was Leningrad, and it took part in the advance through Dvinsk, Ludza, Opochka, Ostrov, and Porkhov. In five days the corps advanced 300 km. Then followed offensive and defensive fighting near Myedved – Werenteni and the attack on Luga and the area south of Staraya Russa. In the period 28 June to 27 August 1941, Gerhard Türke distinguished himself through his circumspection and dazzling leadership qualities in the defensive fighting at Kokini, and the battles in front of Porkhov, on the Luga front, at Borodino and Velikoye-Selo.

June 1941 – driving through East Prussia. Second from the right is Gerhard Türke.

On 11 July 1941 the regimental commander, *Oberst* Gräser, was badly wounded and lost a foot. *Oberstleutnant* Kraßniß took his place. On 8 February 1942, *Oberst* Gräser was awarded the German Cross in Gold for his regiment's success at the start of the Eastern Campaign.

On 20 and 21 August 1941, the division was under orders to attack from west to east and reach the Polist River line approximately 20 km south of Staraya-Russa. Leading the regiment was I Battalion, in particular the 1st Company under the command of *Oberleutnant* Borchert. At 09:00 on 21 August it reached the Polist opposite Borodino. Borchert seized the initiative, crossing the river and establishing a bridgehead. The crossing of the Polist had a major influence on the subsequent advance by the division. The division, including Gerhard Türke's company, crossed the river the same day and was able to advance to the Staraya Russa – Kholm road in order to smash and capture enemy forces retreating from west to north.

For these actions *Oberleutnant* Ernst Borchert (1918-1945) was awarded the Knight's Cross on 29 September 1941.

After the advance on Pola and Lovat, the division moved to the central sector of the Eastern Front. It drove through Roslavl, Iserja, Shanya, and Medyn towards Moscow. Fighting followed near Borovsk, in the Nara bridgehead, and south of Nara Fominsk. In the Yushkovo area, the division was forced to withdraw towards Nara. At the turn of the year 1941-42, the division attacked Tuchkovo and the area on the Rusa. At the beginning of 1942 it was forced to set up defensive positions there.

***Oberleutnant* Türke in Zabrodye, Russia.**

August 1941 – advance in the east.

On 1 February 1942, Gerhard Türke was promoted to *Oberleutnant* and named commander of the 3rd Company of Infantry Regiment 29.

In the spring the division moved to the Orsha area to rest and reequip before being sent to the southern sector. There it took part in the attack across the Don towards Voronezh. The city was taken after heavy fighting. For this *Generalleutnant* Curt Jahn, commander of the 3rd Motorized Infantry Division, was awarded the German Cross in Gold on 18 June 1942.

On 23 August 1942 the division, as part of the XIV Panzer Corps, attacked from the Vyeryachi bridgehead, east of the Don north of Kalach, towards the east. It occupied a sector in the northern blocking line and was the target of fierce attacks by the Russians. Since Orsha the division had covered 2500 km in 82 recognized assault days. It had destroyed more than 1,000 enemy tanks, and Army Flak Battalion 312 was the most successful in the army.

After the 3rd Infantry Division went over to the defensive at the Tatar Wall near Kuzmichi, on 24 November 1942 it received orders to move into the Marinovka sector near Stalingrad. There Türke's military career was to undergo a change that would see him become one of the most highly-decorated members of the division.

Türke experienced the rapid advance into the Soviet Union during the eastern campaign of 1941. The division was part of LVI Army Corps (Motorized) under *Generalleutnant* Erwin von Lewinski, named von Manstein, which was deployed toward Leningrad, in the northern sector of the Eastern Front.

An infantry *Unteroffizier* digs in.

Awarded the Iron Cross, First Class, the Infantry Assault Badge, and the Wound Badge in Black on 21 January 1941, Türke had by then become one of the veteran officers of Infantry Regiment 29. The photos show him with soldiers of his company in Zabrodye, Russia, during the winter of 1941-42.

Spring 1942 in Russia – a break in the fighting, time for mail.

The Fateful Battle for the City on the Volga Begins

After the defeat of the 6th Army – for that is the only way one can characterize its encirclement – no matter what the outcome, and the order for it to remain in that position, the Commander-in-Chief of the *Wehrmacht* initiated measures to relieve the pocket from the outside. *Generaloberst* von Manstein was placed in command of Army Group Don, which had originally been promised to Marshall Antonescu, with orders to advance from the south towards Stalingrad and relieve the 6th Army.

Von Manstein, who had been summoned by Hitler from the headquarters of the 11th Army on 22 November 1942, was briefed on the situation at Stalingrad by *Generaloberst* Maximilian von Weichs (1881-1954, Knight's Cross on 29 June 1940 as *General der Kavallerie* and Commander-in-Chief of the 2nd Army, 731st Oak Leaves on 5 February 1945 as *Generalfeldmarschall* and Commander-in-Chief of Army Group South) on 24 November. He subsequently assumed command of the newly-formed Army Group Don. This consisted of the Rumanian 3rd and 4th Armies, the 6th Army, and the 4th Panzer Army. Under Army Group Don was the Hoth Army Group (Hermann Hoth, 1885-1971, Knight's Cross on 27 October 1939 as commanding general of the VX Army Corps, 25th Oak Leaves on 17 July 1941 as *Generaloberst* and commander of Panzer Group 3, 35th Swords on 15 August 1943 as *Generaloberst* and Commander-in-Chief of the 4th Panzer Army) with the 16th Motorized Division, the 4th Rumanian Army with 2nd army corps, a German battle group, and the 6th and 23rd Panzer Divisions, all of which were east of the Don.

Standing ready west of the Don were two battle groups and the XXXXIV Panzer Corps. On the right of Army Group Don was Army Group A. Also under von Manstein was the 6th Army with four army corps and a panzer corps, plus the Rumanian 3rd Army with two German battle groups and the XVII Army Corps with the attached Rumanian I and II Army Corps. On Army Group Don's right, Army Group B still

General Hans Valentin Hube, commander of the 16th Panzer Division. At 18:35 on 23 August 1942 his units became the first to reach the Volga.

23 August 1942, before Stalingrad. *General* **Hube in his command tank at the head of the 16th Panzer Division. With binoculars is the Commander-in-Chief of** *Luftflotte* **6,** *Generaloberst* **Baron von Richthofen.**

On 30 August 1942, the 4th Panzer Army reached the outer defenses of Stalingrad. The city on the Volga was just 13 kilometers away.

The Historical Background

Hitler first expressed the idea of taking Stalingrad in a directive issued in November 1941, and this took solid form in the summer campaign of 1942. The primary objective of Army Group South (later Army Groups A and B) was to conquer the Caucasus. This was to be achieved in four operations:

1. Breakthrough towards Voronezh (2nd Army and 4th Panzer Army)
2. Destruction of the enemy forces facing the 6th Army west of the Don.

For this purpose:

a) Breakthrough towards the east by the 6th Army from the area east of Kharkov,

b) and simultaneously swing south along the Don by the 4th Panzer Army (moved forward towards Voronezh) in order to destroy the enemy forces west of the Don in conjunction with the 6th Army.

3. Advance to Stalingrad with Army Group B (6th Army and 4th Panzer Army) down the Don to the southeast. Army Group A (17th Army and 1st Panzer Army) from the area east of Taganrog – Artemovski across the lower Donets and then northeast up the Don. Both army groups were supposed to link up in the Stalingrad area and eliminate the city as an armaments and transportation center through occupation or bombardment.

4. Conquest of the Caucasus.

Army Group A, under *Generalfeldmarschall* Wilhelm List (1880-1971, Knight's Cross on 30 September 1939 as *Generaloberst* and Commander-in-Chief of the 14th Army), was given the task of advancing through the Caucasus to the Black Sea and capturing the oil-producing regions of Grozny and Baku. This operation was codenamed "Edelweiss." Hitler's plan would result in an increase in the length of front from the original 800 kilometers to 4100 kilometers. As a result, the force attacking Stalingrad was seriously weakened. *Generaloberst* Franz Halder, head of the army high command (OKH), who voiced opposition to Hitler's plans, was later sent into

had in its ranks the Italian 8th Army, the Hungarian 2nd Army, and the 2nd Army. Army Group Don's orders to the Hoth Army Group were to attack northwards east of the Don and link up with the 6th Army. Army Group Don ordered the 6th Army to make preparations to break out to the south as soon as the Hoth Army Group reached the hills east of Yeriko Krepinski. The Hoth Army group planned to advance along the Kotelnikovo – Stalingrad rail line with its right wing and attempt to link up with the 6th Army southwest of Tundutovo Station. The absence of clear decisions concerning the conduct of the 6th Army were obvious, both in the orders issued by Army Group Don and the plans of the Hoth Army Group. Such a decision was up to the Supreme Commander of the *Wehrmacht*. As was so often the case, no such decision was forthcoming.

According to Army Group Don's orders—which corresponded to those issued by Hitler—the Hoth Army Group was supposed to establish contact with the 6th Army by attacking east of the Don via the shortest route. This meant that, unless the 6th Army first received the order to break out, it had to advance right into the encircling ring. The Hoth Army Group's plans did not go that far, however. Instead, it intended to try to establish contact with the 6th Army southwest of Tundutovo Station. According to this formulation, the Hoth Army Group expected that the 6th Army would come to meet it there. It was a state of affairs that would prove fateful for the 6th Army.

German grenadiers march towards Stalingrad.

6th Army command post. Sitting at the map table is *General* Paulus. On the right, bending over, is *General* Rodenburg, commander of the 76th Infantry Division, and left is operations officer *Oberstleutnant* Eichlepp.

The 16th Panzer Division advancing across the Don steppe in the direction of Stalingrad.

Units of the 6th Army on the road to Stalingrad.

The attack spearheads reached the suburbs of Stalingrad in the second half of September.

early retirement by him (on 24 September 1942) and replaced by *General* Kurt Zeitzler (1895-1963, Knight's Cross on 18 May 1941 as an *Oberst* in the general staff and chief of staff of Panzer Group 1). Thus, the drama of Stalingrad was set to begin.

As envisaged by the supreme command, the primary objective of the summer campaign was not the capture of Stalingrad, but rather the conquest of the Caucasus, with its oil-producing regions. It had been decided, however, that two army groups would first destroy the enemy forces in the area west of Stalingrad in a huge encirclement action. Only then would the conquest of the Caucasus follow. The objective was to destroy for good the Soviets' remaining military power in order to allow the subsequent capture of the oil regions in the Caucasus and access to the Middle East (Hitler Directive No. 41 of 5 April 1942).

When the Soviets withdrew, cleverly using their vast spaces, Hitler was convinced that they were already beaten. He then committed Army Group B under *Generaloberst* Maximilian von Weichs against Stalingrad. Under the code name "Operation *Fischreiher*" (Heron), it was supposed to march on victoriously to the Caspian Sea.

At 02:15 on 28 June 1942, German forces in the east again took the offensive. "Army Group von Weichs" – the 2nd Army (*Generaloberst* von Weichs), the 4th Panzer Army under the command of *Generaloberst* Hoth, and the Hungarian 2nd Army under Colonel-General Gustáv Jány (1883-1947, Knight's Cross on 31 March 1943 as Lieutenant-General and Commander-in-Chief of the Royal Hungarian 2nd Army) – launched an attack against the Briansk Front (Lieutenant-General Golikov) from the Kursk area with eleven infantry divisions and three panzer, three motorized, and ten Hungarian divisions. Supported by *VIII Fliegerkorps* under *Generalleutnant* Martin Fiebig (1891-1947, Knight's Cross on 8 April 1940 as *Oberst* and commander of *Kampfgeschwader 4 "General Wever,"* 168th Oak Leaves on 23 December 1942 as *Generalleutnant* and commanding general of *VIII Fliegerkorps*), they achieved deep penetrations in the area of the Soviet 13th Army of Major-General Pukhov and the 40th Army under Lieutenant-General

Just outside Stalingrad. How to proceed? *Generaloberst* von Richthofen (right) during a visit with General Paulus.

Late summer 1942 – at the objective? General Paulus in Red Square in Stalingrad.

General der Panzertruppe Friedrich Paulus, Commander-in-Chief of the 6th Army.

One of the countless warning signs in the city. It reads: "Entry into the city forbidden. The curious endanger their lives as well as those of their comrades."

Parsegov. On 30 June, the German 6th Army under *General der Panzertruppe* Friedrich Paulus (1890-1957, Knight's Cross on 26 August 1941 as *General der Panzertruppe* and Commander-in-Chief of the 6th Army, 178th Oak Leaves on 15 January 1943 as *Generaloberst*) attacked the southern wing of the Soviet southwest front from the area east of Belgorod. Paulus' force consisted of 16 infantry divisions, two panzer divisions, and one motorized division supported by the *IV Fliegerkorps* under *General der Flieger* Kurt Pflugbeil (1890-1955, Knight's Cross on 5 October 1941 as *Generalleutnant* and commanding general of *IV Fliegerkorps*, 562nd Oak Leaves on 27 August 1944 as

General der Flieger and Commander-in-Chief of *Luftflotte 1*). The attack drove back Major-General Gordov's 21st Army and Lieutenant-General Ryabyshev's 28th Army. On 5 July 1942, Army Group von Weichs reached the Don near Voronezh.

On 6 and 7 July, Army Group South was split into Army Group A (*Generalfeldmarschall* List), including the Rumanian 3rd Army (Colonel-General Ion Dumitrescu, 1889-1977, Knight's Cross on 21 November 1942 as Major-General and commander of the Royal Rumanian 2nd Mountain Division), the 17th Army (*Generaloberst* Richard Ruoff, 1883-1967, Knight's Cross on 30 June 1941 as *General der Infanterie* and commanding general XXII Army Corps), and the 1st Panzer Army (*Generaloberst* Erwin von Kleist, 1881-1954, Knight's Cross on 15 May 1940 as *General der Kavallerie* and commanding general XXII Army Corps, 72nd Oak Leaves on 17 February 1942 as *Generaloberst* and commander of Panzer Group 1, 60th Swords on 30 March 1944 as *Generalfeldmarschall* and Commander-in-Chief of Army Group A), and Army Group B (*Generalfeldmarschall* Fedor von Bock, 1880-1945, Knight's Cross on 30 September 1939 as *Generaloberst* and Commander-in-Chief of Army Group North) with the 2nd Army (*Generaloberst* von Weichs), the Hungarian 2nd Army (Colonel-General Jány), the 6th Army (*General der Panzertruppe* Paulus), and the 4th Panzer Army (*Generaloberst* Hoth).

The first phase of the German 1942 summer offensive ended one day later on 8 July. The Soviet front between the Don and the Donets had been shaken, however, the objective of destroying a large part of the Soviet forces opposite the attack front had not been achieved. On 12 July 1942, the Soviet command formed the Stalingrad Front under Marshall Timoshenko (Lieutenant-General Gordov from 23 July) with four fresh armies.

On 23 July 1942 Hitler issued Directive No 45, which ordered the continuation of "Operation Brunswick"—as "Operation Blue" was named after 30 June—two simultaneous operations against Stalingrad and the Caucasus.

On 28 July 1942, the high command of the Stalingrad Front issued the directive "Not one step back!"

There was bitter fighting for possession of this grain silo in southern Stalingrad.

Near Kalach, in the Don Bend, Russia, autumn 1942. *Leutnant* Stephan (left) and *Leutnant* Wehlmann, members of Türke's company.

Autumn 1942, northern blocking position near Stalingrad. From left: Oblt. Mohr, Oblt. Kesten, and Lt. Schedelgar (adjutant I./IR 29).

The order from Führer Headquarters now affected the divisions under *General der Panzertruppe* Paulus' command: "The 6th Army will take Stalingrad!" Paulus issued the order to attack Stalingrad on 19 August. One day later the 4th Panzer Army initially became bogged down in its attack south of Stalingrad. And in fact, the commander of the 16th Panzer Division, *General* Hans Valentin Hube (1890-1944, Knight's Cross on 1 August 1941 and 62nd Oak Leaves on 16 January 1942 as *Generalmajor* and commander of the 16th Panzer Division, 22nd Swords on 21 December 1942 as *Generalleutnant* and commanding general of XIV Panzer Corps, 13th Diamonds on 20 April 1944 as *General der Panzertruppe* and Commander-in-Chief of the 1st Panzer Army) had already reported by radio on 23 August:

> Battle group Panzer Grenadier Regiment 79 became the first German unit to reach the Volga at 18:35. One company of Panzer Grenadier Regiment 2 occupied Spartakovka. Initially weak enemy resistance later stiffened. Powerful attacks from the north to be expected. VIII Fliegerkorps has given the attack outstanding support.

The Paulus army had reached the farthest point in eastern Russia that any German soldier under arms would ever reach. Hitler's laconic response to XIV Panzer Corps was "16th Panzer Division is to hold its position at all costs."

Two weeks later, German and Rumanian troops entered the suburbs of the city. The attackers suffered heavy casualties in the ensuing street fighting, in some cases losing three-quarters of their fighting strength. The Rumanian troops had only anti-tank guns, but they were incapable of penetrating the frontal armor of the T-34 even from a distance of three meters. Hitler, still of the opinion that the Red Army was incapable of countermeasures that could threaten the *Wehrmacht*, refused to allow himself to be disabused of this notion. With the support of *VIII Fliegerkorps*, the XIV Panzer Corps, under *General der Infanterie* von Wietersheim, drove to the Volga near Rynok, north of Stalingrad. A state of siege was declared for Stalingrad on 25 August. On 10 September, the XXXXVIII Panzer Corps reached the Volga due south of Stalingrad between Yelshanka and Kuperosnoye. Two days later the Soviet High Command placed the defense of Stalingrad in the hands of the 62nd Army under Lieutenant-General Chuikov and elements of the 64th Army under Lieutenant-General Schumilov.

At the end of August, the Soviet High Command renamed the Stalingrad Front the Don Front (Lieutenant-General Rokossovsky) and the Southwest Front

On the way to Klemenskoye.
At left is Gerhard Türke.

the Stalingrad Front (Colonel-General Yeremenko). On 4 October 1942, Army General Zhukov and Colonel-General Vasilevsky, the representative of the Soviet High Command, met with the commander-in-chief of the three fronts to discuss the planned encirclement operations against the German 6th Army.

The Soviets massed eleven armies in preparation for the attack on Stalingrad. The Germans did not discover these movements.

Zhukov and Vasilevsky set 19 November as zero hour for their forces north and south of Stalingrad. The rest would go over to the attack one day later.

At dawn on 19 November 1942, in fog and heavy blowing snow, the Red Army launched its counteroffensive against the German positions with three army corps totaling about 260,000 men, 1,140 tanks, about 17,000 artillery pieces, and more than 1,200 aircraft. The attack quickly developed into a double outflanking and encirclement of all the German forces. The 6th Army, the IV Army Corps of the 4th Panzer Army, the Rumanian 20th Infantry Division, and the Rumanian 1st Cavalry Division – a total of five corps, 14 infantry divisions, three motorized divisions, three panzer divisions, and three Rumanian divisions with approximately 250,000 men, about 1,000 tanks, 1,800 guns, and more than 10,000 vehicles – were thus encircled in the area between the Don and the Volga near Stalingrad.

The two Soviet pincers met near Kalach on 22 November. That evening the following order was issued from Führer Headquarters: "The 6th Army is to form a hedgehog position and wait for relief from outside."

By 23 November 1942, the situation of the XI Army Corps west of the Don became untenable. *Generaloberst* Paulus asked Hitler for freedom of action. The telegram read as follows:

My Führer!
Since the receipt of your telegram of the evening of 22/11 the situation has developed rapidly.

The pocket has not been closed in the southwest and west. There

The 2nd Royal Hungarian Army, under *Lieutenant-General* **Gustáv Jány, advanced out of the Kursk area with eleven infantry divisions, three armored, three motorized, and ten Hungarian divisions. It attacked in the direction of the Briansk Front before turning towards Stalingrad.**

General Friedrich Paulus receives a report outside Stalingrad.

are indications of imminent enemy penetrations there. Ammunition and fuel are running out. Many artillery batteries and anti-tank weapons have no ammunition. Timely, adequate supply is out of the question.

The army will very soon face destruction unless all of our forces are concentrated for a destructive blow against the enemy attacking from the south and west. This requires the immediate withdrawal of all forces from Stalingrad and strong forces from the northern front. An unavoidable consequence must then be a breakout to the southwest, as the eastern and northern fronts thus weakened will be unable to hold.

This will result in the loss of much material, however, we will save most of our valuable fighting men and at least some of our material.

I take full responsibility for this grave report, when I declare that the commanding generals Heitz, Strecker, Hube, and Jaenecke share this assessment of the situation.

Because of the situation I again request freedom of action!

Heil my Führer!
signed Paulus.

Received by the OKH at 23:45 on 23 November: "The enemy is now attacking simultaneously from the west, north (Sirotinskaya), and northeast (loop in the Don west of Schiakiken), and has achieved various penetrations." What Paulus had predicted was coming true. The defenders of Stalingrad were superior to the German attackers.

On 24 November, Paulus received the following telegram from Führer Headquarters:

The 6th Army is temporarily encircled by Russian forces. I intend to concentrate the army in the area Stalingrad North – Kotluban – Hill 137 – Hill 135 – Marinovka-Zybenko-Stalingrad South. The army must be convinced that I will do everything possible to ensure that it is adequately supplied. I know the 6th Army and its brave commander-in-chief and know that it will do its duty.

signed Adolf Hitler

Hitler promised the 6th Army relief. *Reichsmarschall* Hermann Göring (1893-1946, Knight's Cross on 30 September 1939 as *Generalfeldmarschall* and Reich Minister of Aviation and Commander-in-Chief of the Luftwaffe, Grand Cross on 19 July 1940) promised to fly in 300 tons of supplies daily, but when the airlift into the Stalingrad pocket began on 25 November, the *VIII Fliegerkorps* was only able to deliver an average of 95 tons per day. The situation soon became unalterable.

The Battle for Hill 135.1
The Action that Won Türke the Knight's Cross

The 3rd Motorized Infantry Division, led by *Generalmajor* Helmuth Schlömer (1893-1995, Knight's Cross on 2 October 1941 as *Oberst* and commander of Rifle Regiment 5, 161st Oak Leaves on 23 December 1942 as *Generalmajor* and commander of the 3rd Infantry Division) since 30 April 1942, was now moved from the northern front into the Marinovka – Dimitryevka area (the southwest projection of the pocket) to prevent a further advance by the enemy from Kalach and the Krivomusginskaya Station. Point 135 (8 km NNE of Marinovka) was to be turned into a defensive strongpoint. The 29th Motorized Infantry Regiment – part of the 3rd Motorized Infantry Division – had to bear the brunt of the fighting there. The soldiers of the 29th Motorized Infantry Regiment took up positions on Hill 135.1 on 28 November. Among them was *Oberleutnant* Gerhard Türke. From that day the Russians tried to bring about the fall of the "nose of Marinovka." The positions on both sides of Marinovka were important for a breakout to the southwest,

Soldiers running across open ground.

A company commander briefs his platoon leaders on the situation.

Türke had been on Hill 135.1 since 25 November 1942. Strictly speaking, the trigonometric point 135.1 was not a hill, but it was called one. Hills, as they are known in Germany, do not exist in the steppe between the Don and the Volga. Only very gradually, almost imperceptibly, does the terrain form modest rises here and there, which on top are flat as a plate for kilometers. But these hills were tactically significant. They dominated the terrain for kilometers around, usually as far as to where the next hill rose gently. And that was often eight, ten, or twelve kilometers away. Hill 135.1 was approximately twenty kilometers from Stalingrad and 5 km west-southwest of Dimetryevka at the western and southern edge of the city of Marinovka.

The division's sector was 17 kilometers wide and ran from Hill 135.1 on the ridge line at the western edge of the Marinovka training camp west of the Bajrak Ravine, which stretched north from Marinovka to Hills 127.1, 117.8, and 91.3. It then led around Marinovka, then east from Camp Voroshilov along the road to Prudboi.

There Türke and the men under his command were supposed to repulse the fresh attacks expected from the Soviets. The men (members of the 1st Company however. The regiment, indeed the entire division, now had to bear the brunt of the attacks against the defenders of Stalingrad. The 3rd Motorized Infantry Division was now part of the forces under Army High Command 6: five corps, 14 infantry divisions, and two other motorized divisions. At its side stood two Rumanian divisions and a Croatian regiment. They were now attached to Army Group Don within the XIV Panzer Corps. With these troops the division established an all-round defensive position. They had to stop the flood of Soviet attack units that had poured into the empty spaces between the Chir and the Don after the fateful enemy breakthrough. And while the desert of ruins that was Stalingrad gradually became a tomb for the troops fighting there, for countless men in field grey the battlefields became a torture chamber, with constant new versions of suffering.

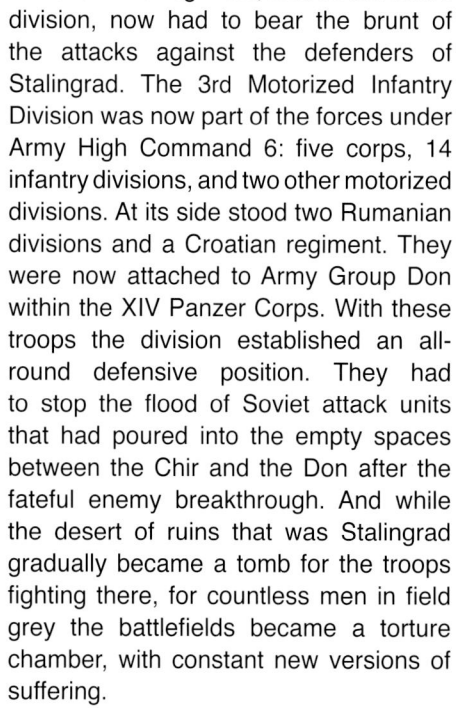

The anti-tank weapons were emplaced a few hundred meters behind the main line of resistance, on the hill's reverse slope. Two heavy anti-aircraft guns of the army flak and heavy anti-tank guns plus a tank company stood ready, and the light and heavy infantry guns, the artillery, and the rocket launchers went into positions from where they could fire with effect on the field in front of the positions. The regiment's sector was thus strongly defended. *Oberleutnant*

The assembly halls of the "Red Barricade" gun factory show traces of the fighting.

of Motorized Infantry Regiment 29) had been under his command since the transfer order. And they didn't have to wait long for the Russian attacks. The first big attack on Marinovka came on 28 November, however, the Germans were able to observe the enemy's preparations. Parts of the town of Marinovka were burning fiercely, and the church steeple had collapsed on itself. Swaths of smoke covered the town. The hill was not spared either. Not with 10 or 15 or 20 tanks, not with rifle companies or battalions, but with 50 to 70 tanks and entire regiments the Russians stormed across the snow-covered steppe and up the slope of Hill 135.1. The grenadiers – a handful compared to the enemy masses – pressed themselves against the cold earth in their holes. They allowed the enemy tanks to overrun them, the infantry to pass, and then they rose from their foxholes to fight.

Enemy tanks were taken out from close range. The anti-tank gunners also did their part. The attackers were repulsed, and none of the enemy reached the main line of resistance. The recent days had demanded everything of the German defenders, and they had been able to defend their hill. There wasn't a bush, not a tree, everywhere only dry, sparse steppe grass, of which only the gray-yellow tips still stuck from the snow.

And everywhere there were burned-out wrecks of tanks.

Hill 135.1 had become the focal point of the Soviet attack. The neighboring companies and battalions had also endured difficult days. But so far luck seemed to have been on the side of the regiment.

Late on the afternoon of 7 December, the Soviets tried to break through along the entire western front, with their greatest effort against the unit on the right of the 376th Infantry Division, and also to take Hill 135.1.

The Russians approached on a front 2,000 meters wide, as if on maneuvers. Large dark objects moved among the men, later turning out to be ammunition carriers and tanks.

For several days in a row they had fought off the enemy's attacks, which had cost the Russians hundreds of dead and many knocked-out tanks.

Tank after tank rolled towards the hill. Once again, as in the previous days, a fierce battle developed.

The Russians succeeded in breaking in between the first and second battalions, achieving a penetration about two kilometers wide and three kilometers deep.

To the last man, and for many of them literally to their last breath, the grenadiers remained in their holes as the tanks approached. But Hill 135.1 and the defense sector under *Oberleutnant* Türke remained in German hands.

The hard winter has begun. Gerhard Türke near Vereya.

Russia, 1942. Move to Hill 135.1 at Marinovka, near Stalingrad. On the left is *Oberleutnant* Türke.

Following his promotion to *Generalmajor*, Helmuth Schlömer took over command of the 3rd Motorized Infantry Division. On 22 December 1942, he was awarded the 161st Oak Leaves for his unit's actions at Stalingrad. The photo shows him as an *Oberst* after receiving the Knight's Cross awarded him on 2/10/1941.

The enemy concentrated his heavy weapons opposite the sector. Thirty tanks, mainly T-34s, rolled toward the foxholes of the German infantry. Artillery, mortars, and multiple rocket launchers pounded Hill 135.1 without letup.

The German anti-aircraft guns which had gone into position to support the neighboring company now went into action.

Then the enemy succeeded in breaking into the position's defensive positions.

In the meantime, the II Battalion of the 8th Motorized Grenadier Regiment had been thrown into the breach. Together with two 20-mm anti-aircraft guns of the 14th Company of the 8th Motorized Grenadier Regiment, it initially sealed off the penetration and then restored the front line. The Russian tanks continued to rampage in the ranks of the Germans. Here and there a grenade exploded, but the Russian tanks kept rolling through the German positions, without infantry but protected by fog and falling snow. Only two made their way back, however. The others were all knocked out by the anti-aircraft guns.

Loyalty and comradeship welded the Stalingrad army into a dangerous force, despite its numerical inferiority. In this photo soldiers are preparing a report for dispatch to the rear. A soldier holds out a spade for the other to write on.

An assault team prepares to move out. German soldiers in the rubble of Stalingrad, which had long since ceased to be a city.

The offensive battle cost the army the best of its forces. Divisions were reduced to regiments. Many good comrades had to be carried to a simple grave in the huge ruined city.

German troops fight their way through a tangle of steel girders and turbines in a blasted power station.

Generalmajor Alexander von Hartmann (1890-1943), commander of the 71st Infantry Division, receives the Knight's Cross from the hands of *Generaloberst* Paulus, Commander-in-Chief of the 6th Army. He was awarded the decoration on 8 October 1942. Hartmann was killed west of Stalingrad on 26 January 1943.

Generaloberst Paulus leaves his command post in Stalingrad.

The Russians were unable to completely overrun the German positions as the defenses were too strong. Every attempt to drive out the defenders had so far failed. *Oberleutnant* Türke and his men had fought with all their strength. Gerhard Türke, the core of the German resistance, was everywhere in those hours as the Russians tried to break into the German positions, inspiring his men by example. Local penetrations into squad and platoon positions were eliminated in hand-to-hand fighting. Wounded soldiers were evacuated to the rear under fire. The Türke Company nevertheless managed to hold onto Hill 135.1 and drive the enemy back.

At that time Gerhard Türke had no idea of the high price in blood his company would have to pay. Now on its own, his company's position had become the main line of resistance.

Unstoppable, he ran from foxhole, mound, and snowdrift to foxhole. Spurred by the zeal of their company commander, his soldiers pulled themselves together and stormed out to meet the Russians. They fought their way forwards meter by meter. With a handful of men Türke drove into the flank of the enemy attack. They quickly opened a narrow corridor.

The Russian mortar fire was ceaseless. A number of stragglers from neighboring companies suddenly appeared and gave covering fire.

Then tanks of the 1st Company of Panzer Battalion 103 arrived. They had rushed from Hill 127.1 and now showered the retreating Russians with fire. Türke and his men continued to advance in the face of heavy enemy fire. Repeatedly taking cover and returning fire, then rising up and charging forward again, they regained a few meters of ground.

The Russians had meanwhile moved up anti-tank guns, but they were engaged and destroyed by the panzers. With élan the infantrymen stormed forwards. They advanced meter by meter, overcoming enemy resistance. Hill 135.1 had not been lost yet. Russian tanks had broken through and were driving towards the neighboring sector. Türke knew that he was in one of the most dangerous situations he had ever faced. Unperturbed, however, and repeatedly

On the horizon is Gumrak airfield, near Stalingrad. For many of the trapped soldiers of the 6th Army, it was the last hope of being supplied or flown out.

An aerial view of the wrecked city of Stalingrad.

motivating the men of his company, he led the charge. Türke was determined to prevent the Russians from rolling up the front no matter what the cost. The enemy drive had to be stopped. Hand-to-hand fighting broke out again.

As evening neared, he had cleared the position of the enemy to the extent possible and forced the Russians on to the defensive.

Enemy pressure against the neighboring company was growing steadily. Three anti-aircraft guns of the 3rd Motorized Artillery Regiment had gone into position there. The gunners accepted the unequal battle against the onrushing tanks. After a brief exchange of fire nine T-34s were burning, but the enemy pressure continued to mount. Two of the anti-aircraft guns had already been knocked out. On account of the great danger, the XIV Panzer Corps sent all available reserves to the point of penetration. The 14th Panzer Division's 64th Motorcycle Battalion and Panzer Battalion 160 were deployed on the right of the regiment's sector. That afternoon the Russians launched a frontal attack against it with about 40 tanks. The panzers fired into the Russian flank until they were out of ammunition. During the night the panzer battalion's battle group remained in reserve east of Hill 135.1. Not until the late evening hours did the sound of battle abate.

Wrecked buildings in southern Stalingrad.

Oberleutnant Türke's grenadiers had again repulsed every enemy attack, with the company commander rushing to the most threatened positions to encourage his men.

There were isolated skirmishes during the night, but no major fighting. The next day the panzer battalion received orders to advance to a position west of the hill. The rumble of tank engines could already be heard in the Türke Company's sector when, suddenly, the tank alarm was sounded. Forty T-34s were driving towards the Panzer IIIs. It appeared that the Russians intended to roll up the company from the flank, and now they ran into the advancing German tanks. A fierce tank battle broke out.

Türke had acted correctly. By pulling back to the prepared stop line and thus withdrawing the front line, he was in part able to master the Russian armada. The Panzer IIIs knocked out four of the attacking T-34s. Another was immobilized in front of a foxhole, with a wrecked track and was abandoned by its crew without firing a shot.

The enemy attack and tank breakthrough had severed the company's communications with the rear. There was also no food. Since two days before, supplies could only reach the front by tank-escorted "convoy."

The fact that the Russians attacked them twice every morning—at exactly the same time—with a rifle company or even an assault team could not conceal the fact that they were digging in several hundred meters to the rear. Meanwhile, the Russian tanks had been completely withdrawn. They were more urgently

A shot-down Bf 109 in the ruins of the city of Stalingrad.

Pitomnik airfield, near Stalingrad. German soldiers clear snow away from a Ju 52 transport.

On 17 December 1942, Gerhard Türke was decorated with the Knight's Cross of the Iron Cross for holding Hill 135.1 near Stalingrad and promoted to *Hauptmann*.

Vorläufiges Besitzeugnis

Der Führer und Oberste Befehlshaber der Wehrmacht

hat

dem _Oberleutnant d.R. Türke,_
Chef 3./Gr.Rgt.(mot)29

das Ritterkreuz des Eisernen Kreuzes

am _17.12.1942_ verliehen.

HQu OKH, den _18. Dezember 1942._

Das Oberkommando des Heeres
i.A.

Generalmajor

needed elsewhere, namely where the Red Army troops themselves had been forced onto the defensive.

General Hube ordered an attack by Panzer Battalion 160 with mounted troops from Motorcycle Battalion 64 on the regiment's right on the night of 10 December. The Türke Company took part in the attack. It regained the former main line of resistance, which was then occupied and defended by Motorcycle Battalion 64. During the night four tanks of the 1st Company also launched a counterattack. Carrying assault troops from the Türke Company, they drove the Russians from their positions, which were then occupied and held by the assault troops. For two more days Türke and his grenadiers held out against determined enemy assaults. Refusing to yield an inch of ground, they ultimately created the conditions necessary for the German counterattack, which took place over two nights. The encircling ring was pierced and the enemy thrown back. The attack culminated in the restoration of the old line. A new defense front was established, with the position held by the Türke Company forming its core. Hill 135.1, near Marinovka, remained firmly in German hands. The battalion, with support from other units of the regiment, had restored contact with the 3rd Company.

The brave decision by Gerhard Türke, the responsible officer, had proven the right one.

It was thanks to the grim determination of the *Oberleutnant* and his grenadiers that the break-in point at that position had been closed so quickly and a larger scale breakthrough by the Russians was prevented.

The decision by the regimental commander, *Oberst* von Beaulieu-Marconnay (1900-1953), not to abandon the sector, to fight off the Russian attacks against the regiment, and to launch a counterattack after all of the penetrations had been eliminated was also critical in achieving the desired outcome.

Oberst Beaulieu-Marconnay. Under his command, IR 29 frustrated every attempt by the enemy to break up the German front for one and a half months. For this he was awarded the Knight's Cross on 20 January 1943. He was taken prisoner in Stalingrad on 31 January 1943 and died in the Krasnopolye camp on 8 October 1953.

Communications with the battalion had been restored, and the regiment's troops had returned to the former main line of resistance. The battalion commander immediately made his way to the *Oberleutnant*'s command post to congratulate him on his decision not to abandon Hill 135.1.

Without *Oberleutnant* Türke and his men, the main line of resistance would have been lost, Hill 135.1 would be in Russian hands, and a larger-scale breakthrough would have taken place. Türke later made his way to the aid station for treatment of the wounds he had suffered in the fighting. He was initially hospitalized.

On 18 December 1942, the news reached Türke that he had been awarded the Knight's Cross of the Iron Cross for his heroic actions on Hill 135.1 near Marinovka, and that he had been promoted to *Hauptmann* with an effective date of 1 December 1942.

He was summoned by the regimental commander, who read to him the following telex:

On 17/12 the supreme commander of the *Wehrmacht* awarded you the Knight's Cross of the Iron Cross.
My congratulations!
Paulus, *Generaloberst*.

Evacuation from the Stalingrad Pocket

Because his wounds required treatment that was not available at the front, Gerhard Türke was flown out of the pocket. He had no idea that by leaving he was escaping an uncertain fate. He was sent to a hospital in Germany and subsequently went on leave to recuperate.

Generalfeldmarschall Paulus, Commander-in-Chief of the 6th Army, during one of his first interrogations by the Russian victors.

General der Flieger Kurt Pflugbeil's *IV. Fliegerkorps* supported the advance towards Stalingrad.

Generalfeldmarschall Fedor von Bock, Commander-in-Chief Army Group B.

Hermann Hoth. With the 2nd Panzer Division, his army group launched the German relief operation towards Stalingrad on 12/12/1942.

For one-and-a-half months Infantry Regiment 29 would frustrate every attempt by the enemy to reduce the German front. For this feat of arms *Oberst* Beaulieu-Marconnay was awarded the Knight's Cross on 20 January 1943. He was taken prisoner in Stalingrad on 31 January 1943 and died in a POW camp in Krasnopolye on 8 October 1953.

At Christmas time the Russians redoubled their efforts to take the town of Marinovka and Hill 135.1.

In Fortress Stalingrad, the 6th Army's heroic struggle went on. On 12 December the Hoth Army Group had launched the operation to relieve Stalingrad spearheaded by the 2nd Panzer Division.

Another panzer division and the 1st Motorized Division were committed on 17 December. By 21 December these forces had reached an area 48 kilometers from Stalingrad. The last attempt at a breakout by the entire 6th Army on 22-23 December could not be given, however, for Hitler refused to give his approval.

Because of the situation in Stalingrad, during the night of 28-29 December 1943 *Generaloberst* Zeitzler urged Hitler to authorize Army Group A to withdraw from the Caucasus. Hitler hesitated, but finally decided to give the order for the army group to retreat from the Caucasus. That same night the army high command transmitted the order.

Geographically, the 6th Army's defense front had changed only a little between 22 November 1942 and 8 January 1943; however, the army was barely able to continue fighting because of shortages of fuel and ammunition and a lack of supplies that weakened the physical state of the troops.

On 8 January 1943, the Russians called upon the 6th Army to surrender. After consulting with the OKH, on Hitler's order Paulus rejected the offer. Paulus still considered a surrender dishonorable.

Fate took its course. Following a heavy artillery bombardment, on 10 January the Russians launched a concentric attack against the western half of the 6th Army's defensive zone. The Soviets broke through near Zybenko in the south, Dimitryevka in the west, and Hill 137 (5 km NW of Rossoshka) in the north. All of the enemy spearheads headed for Pitomnik, the army's principal airfield. Despite Infantry Regiment 29's heroic efforts to hold its ground, on 10 January 1943 it had to abandon its positions after a major Soviet attack broke into the neighboring sector, making it impossible to hold. The regiment had to pay a heavy price in blood.

It soon became apparent that the 6th Army was no longer capable of fighting as an army. Despite a heroic defense by the frontline troops, the enemy could not be stopped tactically or in depth. There were no more mobile reserves due to the lack of fuel and the exhausted state of the men.

Höhe 135,1 - Brennpunkt der Abwehrschlacht
Vom Kampf einer Infanteriedivision im Don-Wolga-Gebiet
Von Kriegsberichter Herbert Rauchhaupt

Im Dongebiet, im Januar

PK. Genau genommen, ist es gar keine Höhe, was man um den trigonometrischen Punkt 135,1 vorfindet, aber es heisst nun einmal so. Höhen in dem Sinne, wie wir sie in Deutschland darunter verstehen, gibt es nicht in dem Steppenland zwischen Don und Wolga. Nur ganz allmählich, kaum dass man es merkt, steigt hier und da das Gelände zu einzelnen, fast unbedeutenden Erhebungen an, die sich oben flach wie ein Teller über kilometerweite Strecken dahindehnen. Auf ihnen steht kein Baum und kein Strauch, sondern wie überall gedeiht auch hier nur das dürre, spärliche Steppenkraut, von dem jetzt seit Wochen nur noch die graugelben Spitzen aus der Schneedecke hervorragen. Gerade diese kahle Leere aber gibt diesen Höhen entscheidende taktische Bedeutung. Auf weite Entfernung im Umkreis beherrschen sie das Gelände, meist bis dorthin, wo die nächste Höhe sanft ansteigt. Und das sind oft acht, zehn und zwölf Kilometer.

Über die Höhe 135,1 nun verläuft jene Abwehrstellung, an der vor Wochen die sowjetische Winteroffensive endgültig zum Stehen kam. Wie gegen unsere gesamte Front im Don-Wolga-Gebiet, so brandeten Tage hindurch mit Hunderten von Panzern und einer noch unübersehbaren Zahl von Schützendivisionen die Wellen der massierten feindlichen Angriffe gegen die Höhe 135,1 an. Als dem Gegner trotz rücksichtslosem Einsatz von Menschen und Material an keiner Stelle der Durchbruch gelang, änderte er die Taktik und griff nicht mehr konzentrisch an, sondern löste seine grossangelegte Operationen in einzelne, dafür aber um so heftiger geführte Vorstösse gegen die Stellen der deutschen Hauptkampflinie auf, an denen er uns schwach glaubte oder denen ein besonderer taktischer Wert zukam. Das bedeutete, dass es an manchen Abschnitten sehr bald schon wieder ruhig wurde und die Fronten im Stellungskrieg erstarrten. Schliesslich blieben noch zwei Schwerpunkte übrig, an denen die Bolschewisten mit unverminderter Wucht anrannten, und zuletzt war es nur noch eine Stelle. Diese aber hiess: Höhe 135,1!

Als sich am 28. November deutsche Soldaten auf Höhe 135,1 erstmalig zur Verteidigung einrichteten, fanden sie nichts vor als diese trostlose, kahle Fläche, auf der sich ihnen keine auch noch so bescheidene Deckung bot, kein Erdloch, kein Graben, kein Unterstand, nichts. Das alles — ihre gut ausgebaute Winterstellung — hatten sie verlassen müssen, als sie die oberste Führung in diesen entscheidenden Abschnitt der Abwehrfront dirigierte, an dem von Anfang an der Brennpunkt der gesamten Abwehrschlacht zu erwarten war. Im Schutze der Dunkelheit glitten Spitzhacke und Spaten in die hartgefrorene Erde, so dass in aller Eile wenigstens ein paar behelfsmässige Panzerdeckungslöcher entstanden. Wenige hundert Meter hinter der Hauptkampflinie, auf den Hinterhang der Höhe, fuhren die panzerbrechenden Waffen auf — zwei schwere Heeresflak-, mittlere und schwere Panzerjägerkanonen —, eine Panzerkompanie stand einsatzbereit, und die leichten und schweren Infanteriegeschütze, die Artillerie und die Werfer gingen in einigen Schluchten so in Stellung, dass sie ohne Schwierigkeiten in das Vorgelände der Höhe 135,1 wirken konnten. So war der Abschnitt des Grenadierregiments stark gesichert. Die Bolschewisten mochten kommen....

Und sie kamen! Nicht mit 10 oder 15 oder 20 Panzern, nicht mit Schützenkompanien und -bataillonen, sondern mit 50 oder 60 oder 70 Kampfwagen und ganzen Regimentern Infanterie ergossen sie sich über die verschneite Steppe und den jenseitigen Hang der Höhe 135,1 herauf. Die Grenadiere, eine Handvoll im Vergleich zu diesen Massen des Feindes, pressten sich in ihren Löchern an die kalte Erde. Sie kannten das, wenn die Stahlkolosse anrollten, waren in Hunderten von Gefechten für immer panzerfest geworden. Dann donnerten die sowjetischen Kampfwagen an ihnen vorbei und über sie hinweg, und während sie sich wieder erhoben und MG-Garben zwischen die Rudel feindlicher Infanterie mähten, entbrannte in ihrem Rücken der Kampf zwischen unseren panzerbrechenden Waffen — die Panzer mit eingerechnet — und den Kampfwagen des Gegners. Das Ergebnis war, dass kein bolschewistischer Schütze unsere Hauptkampflinie erreichte, dass aber auch keiner der sowjetischen Panzer zu seinen eigenen Linien zurückkehrte.

So ging es Tag für Tag unvermindert weiter, als sei diesmal die Reserven des Feindes an Material, besonders an Panzern, unerschöpflich. Jetzt ballte der Gegner vor der Abschnitt auch seine schweren Waffen zusammen und trommelte mit Artillerie, Granatwerfern und Salvengeschützen oft stundenlang ohne Unterbrechung auf Höhe 135,1 in der Hoffnung, beim nächsten Angriff eine moralisch angeschlagene Truppe vorzufinden. Dann schossen auch unsere Rohre heraus, was sie hergaben, zerschlugen die feindlichen Bereitstellungen oder legten Sperrfeuer in die Annäherungsräume der Bolschewisten. An diesen Tagen glich das Gelände von früh bis abend einem einzigen Vulkan von krepierenden Granaten und Wurfgeschossen, und 20, 30 Kilometer weit war an der deutschen Abwehrfront der Kanonendonner von Höhe 135,1 zu hören. Aber durchgekommen sind sie nicht!

Nur ein einziges Mal, bei einem seiner letzten schweren Panzerangriffe, gelang dem Feind vorübergehend ein Durchbruch durch unsere Abwehrstellung. Bis zum letzten Mann und viele von ihnen buchstäblich bis zum letzten Atemzuge blieben beim Anrollen der Sowjetpanzer die Grenadiere in ihren Deckungslöchern liegen, und erst auf Befehl wurde ein schmaler Abschnitt der Hauptkampflinie geräumt. Aus eigenem Entschluss sammelte ein Kompanieführer, Oberleutnant Türke, sofort sämtliche verfügbaren Kräfte und schirmte mit ihnen die durch den feindlichen Stoss aufgerissene Flanke ab, um ein Aufrollen der Front zu verhindern. Tage hindurch wehrten sich diese Grenadiere verbissen gegen den eingedrungenen, weiterhin angreifenden Feind. Nicht einen Schritt wichen sie mehr zurück und schufen so die Voraussetzung für den deutschen Gegenangriff, der in zwei nächtlichen Unternehmungen durchgeführt wurde und dessen Erfolg in der Wiederherstellung der alten Linie gipfelte.

Die drei Wochen Abwehrkampf haben die Höhe 135,1 gezeichnet. So weit man an diesem grauen Wintertag auch blicken kann, ganz gleich ob feindwärts oder rückwärts — überall ragen die ausgebrannten Trümmer abgeschossener und gesprengter Sowjetpanzer, meist vom Typ T 34, als verrusste und verrostete Schrotthaufen aus dem verschneiten Steppenland. Am dichtesten stehen sie auf der Hochfläche beieinander, und hier liegen auch noch reihenweise die Leichen gefallener Bolschewisten dazwischen — ausgebootete Panzerbesatzungen und aufgesessene Schützen, die von den Garben deutscher Maschinengewehre und 2-Zentimeter-Flakgeschütze niedergemäht worden sind. Höhe 135,1 ist ein riesiger Panzerfriedhof geworden, das Leichenfeld erstreckt sich bis weit hinaus vor unsere Hauptkampflinie, wo die sowjetische Infanterie zu Hunderten, wenn nicht zu Tausenden in den Tod marschiert ist.

Aber nicht allein die Kämpfe stellten hier unmenschliche Anforderungen an die Truppe, sondern hinzu kam noch eine Unzahl von Schwierigkeiten, die unsere Soldaten überwinden mussten, ehe überhaupt der Kampf mit dem Gegner begann.

Ja, es hat hier Stunden gegeben, in denen sich sämtliche Widerstände der Welt gegen die deutschen Soldaten verbündet zu haben schienen. Bald schwankte die Temperatur zwischen zwei Grad Wärme und 15 Grad Kälte, bald regnete es in Strömen und wenige Stunden später froren die durchnässten und verdreckten Wintersachen den Soldaten am Leibe stocksteif. Die Nächte wieder waren meist ohne Sterne, so dass in dem verschneiten Steppengelände, in dem auf kilometerweite Entfernungen ein Quadratmeter dem anderen wie ein Ei dem anderen gleicht, die Melder ohne jede Orientierungsmöglichkeit oft stundenlang umherirrten, ehe sie die Gefechtsstände fanden. Und, als nach dem Durchbruch der feindlichen Panzer die Verbindungen nach rückwärts vorübergehend abgeschnitten waren, blieb auch die Verpflegung aus und konnte schliesslich nur mit Hilfe eines von Panzern gesicherten «Geleitzuges» nach vorn gelangen.

Aber heute ist den Bolschewisten auch bei Höhe 135,1 die Lust am Angreifen vergangen. Die Tatsache, dass sie jeden Morgen zweimal — dazu noch zu ihren festen Zeiten — mit einer Kompanie Schützen oder auch nur mit einem Stosstrupp anrennen, kann nicht darüber hinwegtäuschen, dass sie einige hundert Meter weiter rückwärts deutlich sichtbar schanzen und sich auch hier wie überall längs der deutschen Abwehrfront zur Verteidigung, zum Stellungskrieg einrichten. Ihre Panzer haben sie völlig abgezogen. Sie brauchen sie an anderer Stelle dringender — dort nämlich, wo sie inzwischen selbst in die Abwehr geraten und starke deutsche Verbände zum grossen Entlastungsstoss angetreten sind.

Auf Höhe 135,1 hielten und halten auch heute noch Grenadiere, Panzer, Panzerjäger und Artillerie einer brandenburgischen motorisierten Infanterie-Division die Stellung, derselben Division, die wegen hervorragender Waffentaten wiederholt im Bericht des Oberkommandos der Wehrmacht genannt worden ist.

Reception at Home

Meanwhile, Gerhard Türke was receiving a warm reception while on convalescence leave. At the invitation of the mayor in his home town of Heinersdorf, the residents gathered in the *Hotel zur Eisenbahn*. The gaily decorated room could barely hold all the people who came to take part in the celebration. Mayor Höhne gave the welcoming speech, praising the troops in Stalingrad in general and Knight's Cross wearer Gerhard Türke in particular. All of Heinersdorf was proud of its Knight's Cross winner. News of the award appeared in the paper within days of Türke receiving the decoration.

There were many words and much praise for Gerhard Türke. He received it all with a staid sense of calmness, for he was truly a modest man. What he had done was not out of a desire to make himself out to be a hero or accomplish something glorious—he only did what he had to when worst came to worst. He owed it to his soldiers.

The speech by the mayor was followed by an address by the party's local group leader. Then he was offered honorary membership in the National-Socialist Warrior's Society. But what moved him much more deeply than all the honors and congratulations was the fact that his men were still moving towards an uncertain fate in the Battle of Stalingrad.

At one of the city's airfields, wounded Stalingrad fighters are loaded on to a Ju 52 in preparation for evacuation. Gerhard Türke escaped the inferno of captivity in one such machine.

Dr. Goebbels in casual conversation with the brave soldiers. On the left is Gerhard Türke.

Ritterkreuzträger aus dem Handwerk

Hauptmann Gerhard Türke

wurde am 1. Mai 1914 als Sohn eines Zimmermanns in Heinersdorf (Kr. Lebus) geboren. Nach dem Besuch der Volks- und Mittelschule und abschließendem Abitur auf der Staatlichen Aufbauschule in Fürstenwalde genügte er 1933 seiner Arbeitsdienstpflicht und schied dort als Truppführer aus. Als Zugführer nahm er am Polenfeldzug teil, wo ihm das EK. II verliehen wurde. Gegen Frankreich wurde er als Kompanieführer eingesetzt und erhielt das EK. I, das Infanterie-Sturm- und Verwundeten-Abzeichen. Im Feldzug gegen die Sowjets war er überall dabei, wo heiße Kämpfe tobten; schon bald erhielt er das Deutsche Kreuz in Gold. Bei den schweren Kämpfen im Raum um Stalingrad verteidigte er seine Stellung auch dann noch mit eiserner Ent-

One of the many newspaper articles on the awarding of the Knight's Cross to Gerhard Türke.

Wearing all his decorations, Türke in a wedding photo.

Destruction of the 6th Army and Its Rebirth

On 20 January 1943, the 6th Army surrendered in Stalingrad after putting up desperate resistance. *Generaloberst* Paulus, who the day before had been promoted to *Generalfeldmarschall* and on 15 January 1943 had become the 178th German soldier to receive the Knight's Cross with Oak Leaves, halted the now pointless battle on the Volga after Hitler again refused to allow him to surrender on the 26th.

The 90,000 survivors of the original 200,000 men of the 6th Army went into captivity with the *Generalfeldmarschall*. Only a few thousand would survive the long years of captivity to see their homeland again.

Among the prisoners were the men of the 1st Company of Infantry Regiment 29. In the course of the fighting in Stalingrad, the regiment reported 606 of its men missing, and the fate of most of these men remains a mystery to this day.

For the German Reich, however, this disastrous defeat marked the beginning of the end. The tide of the war had turned.

Already on 26 January 1943, the organizational department of the OKH began drafting notes on the reformation of the divisions of a "new" 6th Army.

Article 3d called for the formation of a new 3rd Motorized Infantry Division. To the extent possible, the 6th Army was to be created using convalescents from the "old" 6th Army, which had been destroyed in Stalingrad. At the end of March 1943, the new division was created in the Pyrenees as the 3rd Panzer Grenadier Division. The 386th Motorized Infantry Division from Defense District III, to which many members of the old division had been transferred from replacement units, formed the basis of the new division.

Oberst Hans Hecker (here as a *Generalmajor*) succeeded *Generalleutnant* Gräser as commander of the 3rd Panzer Grenadier Division on 28 April 1944. He had earlier received the Knight's Cross on 5 August 1940 as an *Oberstleutnant* and commander of Motorized Pioneer Battalion 29.

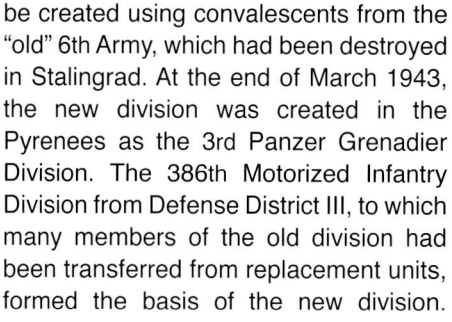

Fritz-Hubert Gräser, who had been promoted to *Generalleutnant* on 1 March 1943, was named division commander, leaving his position as commander of the 29th Motorized Infantry Division.

General Gräser saw to it that as many former division members as possible were placed in their old positions as unit commanders. Thus, during formation of the new division on 1 June 1943, *Hauptmann* Türke arrived in Biarritz, France, where he was given command of the I Battalion of the 29th Motorized Grenadier Regiment, which had been formed from the 63rd Motorized Infantry Regiment.

Before going to France, on 17 March 1943 he and a group of frontline soldiers who had escaped the Stalingrad Pocket were the guests of Reich Minister Dr. Goebbels in Berlin.

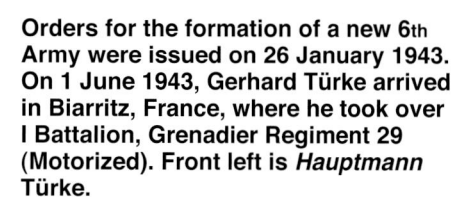

Orders for the formation of a new 6th Army were issued on 26 January 1943. On 1 June 1943, Gerhard Türke arrived in Biarritz, France, where he took over I Battalion, Grenadier Regiment 29 (Motorized). Front left is *Hauptmann* Türke.

Action in Italy

On 10 July 1943, Allied forces under the overall command of General Eisenhower landed on the island of Sicily in an operation code named "Husky." This marked the beginning of the battle for Fortress Europe.

137 glider trains approached the Sicilian coast. 260 Douglas Dakota transports carrying 2,700 paratroopers of the 82nd Airborne Division set course for the island. From the sea more than 300,000 men approached Sicily, preparing to make the jump to Europe.

A fleet of 3,000 ships formed up at the designated rendezvous points in the Mediterranean and, under German artillery fire, delivered troops, guns, tanks, and other war materiel to the coast. While the American paratroopers landed behind the German lines and began fighting, British troops began coming ashore near Gela. Despite fierce German resistance, the Allies pursued their objective of rolling up the German front from the south with determination. Sicily had to be taken to provide closer communications with the supply bases in North Africa. Only thus could the German front be shaken.

Facing this armada on the Axis side was the Italian 6th Army under General Guzzoni with the XII and XVI Army Corps (4th, 26th, 28th, and 54th Infantry Divisions, the 202nd, 206th, 208th, 213th, and 222nd Coastal Defense Divisions), plus the "Hermann Göring" Panzer Division and the 15th Panzer Grenadier Division.

The landings were supported by gunfire from Allied warships. The 15-inch guns of six battleships pounded the Italian positions and fortifications without letup.

Poor Italian morale, the rebellious Italian officer corps, and the great confusion did not make things easier for the German troops. Doggedly they held their positions. But the battle for Sicily had become hopeless. Italian resistance was spotty.

In the first two days the Allies put ashore 80,000 men, 7,000 vehicles, and about 300 tanks. Against such an overwhelming force, the troops of the Commander-in-Chief South, *Generalfeldmarschall* Kesselring (1885-1960, Knight's Cross on 30 September 1939 as *General der Flieger* and commander of *Luftflotte 1*, 78th Oak Leaves on 25 February 1942 as *Generalfeldmarschall* and commander of *Luftflotte 2* and Commander-in-Chief South, 15th Swords on 18 July 1942, 14th Diamonds on 19 July 1944 as *Generalfeldmarschall* and Commander-in-Chief Southwest, also Commander-in-Chief of Army Group C) had no chance.

The western half of Sicily was taken by troops of the American 7th Army under General Patton. The Allies had taken the first step towards the capture of Italy. Total Allied casualties were about 20,000 men killed, wounded, and missing, but success was on their side.

An evacuation of the island was begun; nevertheless, 135,000 German and Italian soldiers became prisoners of war and 260 tanks, 502 guns, and 1,691 aircraft were destroyed or captured. On 17 July *General der Panzertruppe* Hube, commanding general of the XIV Panzer Corps, which had been sent to the island, assumed command of all German troops on Sicily.

On 22 July the American 7th Army took Palermo. On 25 July Mussolini, who had offered to step down, was arrested. The Italian kings asked Marshall Badoglio to form a new government, and the new head of state declared his intention to fight on at Germany's side.

Leutnant d.R. Norbert Semrau, a platoon leader in the 1st Company of Motorized Grenadier Regiment 29, was awarded the Knight's Cross on 6 April 1944 for holding a hill north of Aprilia, Italy, and ended the war as a *Hauptmann der Reserve*.

After the division was moved to Italy, it conducted training in the Chiusi-Lake Bolsena area. Here Gerhard Türke (center) is seen with members of his staff.

August 1944 in Italy: Gerhard Türke with *Hauptmann* Apel, wearer of the German Cross in Gold.

the first attack, but was forced to make a gradual fighting retreat. The LXXVI Panzer Corps also fell back step-by-step. The German units in the Nicastro—Catanzaro area halted the enemy, however. *Generalfeldmarschall* Kesselring wanted to ascertain the precise direction of advance of the Allied landing force before committing the 16th Panzer Division.

On the same day, in Cassibile, Sicily, the Italians secretly agreed to a cease fire with the Allies. It was announced by General Eisenhower on 5 September.

Meanwhile, on 9 September the American 5th Army under General Clark landed near Salerno; however, it also ran into stiff German opposition. The German defenders had the advantage, and were able to lay down accurate fire on the landing from hilltop positions. The first wave of landing units was beaten back by armored units of the XXIV Panzer Corps.

The Battle of Salerno, in which American marine units also took part, raged on. Salerno was soon encircled but did not fall.

In position there was the 16th Panzer Division under the command of *Generalmajor* Rudolf Sieckenius (1896-1945, Knight's Cross on 17 September 1941 as *Oberstleutnant* and commander of Panzer Regiment 2). Spread out over 40 kilometers of front, it was able to prevent a rapid advance, but could not halt the enemy.

The battle came to an end on 18 September and the Allied advance continued.

German countermeasures in the event of a rebellion by Italy, or "Case Axis" – preparations for which had been in place for weeks – had meanwhile begun. Rome was occupied on 10 September, after the Italian Motorized Corps under General Carboni was overpowered or disarmed. The 3rd Panzer Grenadier Division took part in the disarming of the Italian troops.

Battles against the Allied Invasion Forces

The 3rd Panzer Grenadier Division had been transferred to Italy at the end of June-beginning of August 1943. From

Final peaceful days with comrades in Rome.

On 1 August *General* Hube assumed command of all German and Italian troops in Sicily.

But the Allied advance could not be stopped. After heavy fighting the "Hermann Göring" Panzer Division was forced to give up the city of Catania. The supreme command gave orders for "Operation *Lehrgang*," the evacuation of Sicily, to be set in motion. Approximately 40,000 German troops, including 4,444 wounded, 9,600 vehicles, 47 tanks, 94 guns, and more than 2 000 tons of ammunition and fuel, plus about 15,000 tons of other materiel were ferried to southern Italy, along with 62,000 Italian troops with 227 vehicles and 41 guns.

The fighting on Sicily ended on 17 August 1943. By then the Allies had also occupied Sardinia and Corsica.

Meanwhile, Allied troops had also landed on the Italian mainland, causing the German front to crumble. The battle for the Italian mainland had begun. On 3 September troops of the British 8th Army under General Montgomery landed on the southern tip of Calabria. The 29th Panzer Grenadier Division was ordered to halt

July to August it trained in the Chiusi – Lake Bolsena area. The division had been released from the formation of the (new) 6th Army.

Since the end of July, the division had been under the Commander-in-Chief South. It was part of the 14th Army under *Generaloberst* Eberhard von Mackensen (1889-1969, Knight's Cross as *General Der Kavallerie* and commanding general of the III Motorized Army Corps on 27 July 1941, 95th Oak Leaves on 26 May 1942 as commanding general of the III Panzer Corps). With the 2nd Parachute Division it moved from the north and southwest towards Rome.

After Italy's surrender, the 3rd Panzer Grenadier Division was transferred south, where it was attached to the XIV Panzer Corps under *Generalleutnant* Fridolin von Senger und Etterlin (1891-1963, Knight's Cross on 8 February 1943 as *Generalmajor* and commander of the 17th Panzer Division, since October 1943 commanding general of the XIV Panzer Corps, previously *Wehrmacht* Commander in Sicily since June 1943 and from August 1943 on Sardinia and Corsica, 439th Oak Leaves on 5 April 1944 as *General der Panzertruppe* and commanding general of the XIV Panzer Corps). With three divisions, the corps was fully engaged against the enemy. These were the 3rd Panzer Grenadier Division in Abruzzi, the 90th Panzer Grenadier Division, and the 95th and 305th Infantry Divisions, which were then reinforced by retreating forces of the 10th Army and 1st Parachute Division that had pulled back in heavy fighting against the British 78th Infantry Division. Meanwhile, Kesselring had ordered the evacuation of the port and city of Naples by German troops. He had searched for a proper defense line and selected the Apennine Mountains and Abbruzi. The "Gustav Line" stretched across the peninsula from west to east. Kesselring took advantage of Italy's natural obstacles. The country could best be defended in the two regions in which the mountains extended between the Tyrrhenian Sea and the Adriatic. In the north, Army Group C held up the Allies between La Spezia and Rimini, and south of Rome between Gaeta and Pescara. In that sector the road to Rome was bordered near the Cassino narrows by the Monti Aurunci on one side and Monte Cairo on the other. Both mountains were more than 1,500 meters high. In the center of the defense line were the even higher mountains Monti Miletto, Petroso, and the 2795-meter high Monte Malella. From there the mountains dropped sharply to the Adriatic, leaving the Allies just a narrow strip of coast from Bari to Rimini on which to advance.

The many fast-flowing rivers in the area provided another obstacle to the Allied advance. Kesselring exploited all these advantages and placed ten divisions in the defense line. However, it was a German counterattack towards Salerno that allowed the defense line to be established.

The attacking Allied forces came no further. Using all the means at his disposal and improvisation, Kesselring had prevented an impending breakthrough.

At the beginning of 1944 the Allied advance came to a halt. The battle for the forward position in the "Gustav Line" began on 3 January. The German defenders exploited the advantages provided by the terrain and held off the attackers until 15 January. Not until that day did French troops under General Juin take Monte Santa Croce. The stalled advance led the Allies to undertake a landing in the German rear.

On the night of 22 January 1944, nine transport ships and 226 landing craft carrying 68,886 troops, 508 guns, and 237 tanks of the American VI Corps under Major-General Lucas headed for Anzio-Nettuno Bay, south-southwest of Rome. In the early morning hours they came ashore about 8 km north of Anzio and about 50 km south of Rome. The force was supposed to immediately break through towards Rome, but instead of advancing it paused to assemble. With only elements of the "Hermann Göring" Panzer Division available, *Generalfeldmarschall* Kesselring took units from the 10th Army, which was just being formed, and sealed off the area. On the German side of the beachhead, by 26 January the 3rd Panzer Grenadier Division, under *Generalleutnant* Gräser, had been inserted into the western part of the line, while the 4th Parachute Division had occupied the coastal sector. The 65th Infantry Division, which arrived

10 June 1944 in Italy. The last day in Rome before returning to combat.

quickly and seized Hill 80 and the town of Carroceto from the enemy in a series of battles, manned its positions west of the Anzio – Albano road on 28 January, while the 715th Infantry Division covered the Alban Mountains and the 362nd Infantry Division established a new main line of resistance on both sides of Cisterna.

Under the command of *General* Alfred Schlemm (1894-1986, Knight's Cross on 11 June 1944 as *General der Flieger* and commanding general of I Parachute Corps), the *XI Fliegerkorps* became a mobile fire brigade in the invasion area.

The air corps – a mixture of units from the "Hermann Göring" Panzer Division, the 26th Panzer Division, the 3rd and 90th Panzer Grenadier Divisions, 4th Parachute Division, and several guard and alert units – had become a potent instrument.

The German defenders also pounded the Allied landing force with coastal batteries and heavy weapons. From far behind the front two 280-mm K5 "Leopold" railroad guns, in well-camouflaged and difficult-to-locate positions beside the railroad tracks, also shelled the enemy. They inflicted heavy casualties on the attackers.

BESITZZEUGNIS

DEM __Hauptmann__
(DIENSTGRAD)

__Gerhard Türke__
(VOR- UND FAMILIENNAME)

__I./Gren.Rgt. (mot) 29__
(TRUPPENTEIL)

VERLEIHE ICH FÜR TAPFERE TEILNAHME AN __30__ NAHKAMPFTAGEN

DIE __2__. STUFE DER NAHKAMPFSPANGE

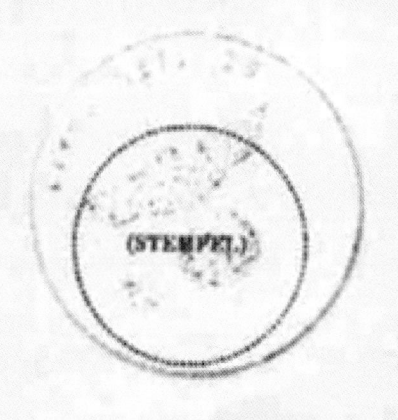

Rgt.Gef.Std., den 13.6.1944
(ORT UND DATUM)

(UNTERSCHRIFT)

Oberst und Rgt.-Kommandeur
(DIENSTGRAD UND DIENSTSTELLUNG)

(STEMPEL)

Generalmajor Walter Denkert took over command of the division on 5 October 1944.

The English, who held a line from Aprilia and Carocetto to Campoleone, 22 km north of Anzio, were also driven back.

On 30 January *Hauptmann* Roßmann, commander of I Battalion, 29th Motorized Grenadier Regiment, was killed during an assault near Osteriaccia. Gerhard Türke subsequently took over his position.

On 7 February the 3rd Panzer Grenadier Division drove the enemy back another three kilometers.

On 16 February, the Germans launched their counterattack against the Anzio-Nettuno beachhead, which had been in preparation since the end of January. The goal was to drive the Americans into the sea. The LXXVI Panzer Corps, under the command of *General der Panzertruppe* Traugott Herr, and the I Parachute Corps under *General der Flieger* Schlemm gained a little ground, but then became bogged down.

On 27 February Hitler ordered another attack on the Anzio-Nettuno beachhead.

The attack began on 29 February, but losses were so high that the attack was not a decisive success. Unwilling to accept the responsibility for such bloodshed, Kesselring stopped the attack on 1 March. The Allies marched deeper into Italy. In May the 3rd Panzer Grenadier Division was located near Aprilia.

At the end of May *Hauptmann* Türke and his battalion were in the area near Cavaliere.

After briefly taking over the duties of regimental commander, *Hauptmann* Gerhard Türke again took over command of the I Battalion and occupied new positions between the Canaliere farmstead and Ponte Loreib.

In recent days the Allied troops, under the command of General Clark, had changed their main direction of attack and were marching towards the Alban Mountains. Their main objective was Rome. English troops joined the battle south of Aprilia. Weaker enemy forces took Artena, and then, supported by tanks, ran into the defense sector of I Battalion, 29th Motorized Grenadier Regiment. The enemy succeeded in approaching to within 1,000 meters of the 1st company in battalion strength. Enemy reconnaissance aircraft were constantly overhead, suggesting that preparations were under way for an attack in Fosso Presciano. But apart from increasingly heavy artillery and mortar fire and several weak reconnaissance probes, there was no major fighting. The new defense line ran as follows: on the right was the II Battalion of the Infanterie-Lehr Regiment, then the III Battalion. Beside it was *Hauptmann* Türke's battalion, then the Parachute Assault Battalion under *Hauptmann* Genz (1916-2000, Knight's Cross on 14 June 1941 as company commander *1./Fsch.Jäg.Sturm.Rgt.*). On its left was Battle Group Wehrmann with Field Replacement Battalions 3 and 165.

For days no food or water had reached the front lines. Türke's men were dying of thirst; nevertheless, the grenadiers held their position and put up heroic resistance.

On 29 May 1944, the enemy launched fresh heavy attacks in the regiment's sector. Türke himself stood like a rock amid the waves, shouting commands and orders. Türke knew that there were twelve

Türke with a member of his regimental headquarters.

Members of Türke's regimental headquarters staff.

enemy tanks in or in front of the position. Then two assault guns rushed from the III Battalion. In a matter of minutes a young *Fahnenjunker-Unteroffizier* knocked out five Shermans. After that there was no holding for the Americans. The rest of the American tanks fled back to their starting position.

The 2nd Company was now in the main line of resistance between the 1st Company and the 11th Company of Grenadier Regiment 8, which had been placed under Türke's command. The grenadiers fought fiercely. By about 09:30 the situation was completely cleared up, and the main line of resistance was again firmly in the battalion's hands. Under the command of Gerhard Türke, the battalion had repulsed a major attack and inflicted heavy casualties on the enemy.

All day long the battalion's sector lay under harassing fire, but there were no fresh attacks. The following night was quiet, apart from light artillery and mortar fire. Beginning at 05:00, however, the ground again began to tremble. Heavy artillery fire of all calibers began falling on the Türke Battalion's sector. Again dust and smoke shrouded the main line of resistance. All telephone and radio communications were out. Ceaseless fighter-bomber attacks prevented the German artillery from giving support. One of the two available assault guns broke down and had to be towed away.

Most threatened was the sector on the left wing, manned by 11th Company, Grenadier Regiment 8. Enemy tanks moved in and shot up everything that moved. Meanwhile, German defensive fire had begun striking the enemy and the first casualties fell.

Four Sherman tanks came driving out of a depression and approached at high speed. Following them were infantry, trying to achieve the decisive breakthrough. At about 10:00 the attack was halted by the grenadiers, whose fire had inflicted heavy losses on the enemy.

Once again, *Hauptmann* Türke had achieved a defensive success. The 1st and 2nd Companies in particular distinguished themselves through their steadfastness. Casualties in Türke's battalion had been heavy, however.

During the midday hours, the enemy launched a weaker attack against the battalion's positions. All day long the main line of resistance and the battalion's sector lay under increasingly heavy artillery and mortar fire. By the time dusk fell, Türke's command post had been wrecked. The following day, the enemy again tried several times to overrun the main line of resistance with tank support. These attacks were also repulsed, however, and the positions remained in German hands. Under *Hauptmann* Türke the battalion had achieved a proud defensive success. The enemy suffered heavy losses.

On 4 June 1944, Army Group Southwest's front between the 14th Army, under *Generaloberst* von Mackensen, and the 10th Army of *Generaloberst* Heinrich-Gottfried Baron von Vietinghoff, nee Scheel (1887-1952, Knight's Cross on 24 June 1940 as *General der Panzertruppe* and commanding general XIII Army Corps, 456th Oak Leaves on 16 April 1944 as *Generaloberst* and Commander-in-Chief 14th Army), was torn open. All that remained of the entire 14th Army, which faced the threat of destruction, were four battered divisions:

4th Parachute Division
65th Infantry Division
3rd Panzer Grenadier Division
362nd Infantry Division

For several weeks the three divisions in the line on either side of Empoli stopped the American attacks. At the end of June, however, their remnants began pulling back across the Tiber, east of Lake Bracciano and Lake Bolsena, through Siena to the Arno Position west of Florence.

On 28 April 1944, *Oberst* Hans Hecker (Knight's Cross on 5 August 1940 as *Oberstleutnant* and commander of Motorized Pioneer Battalion 29) relieved *Generalleutnant* Gräser as commander of the 3rd Panzer Grenadier Division. Gräser left to take over as commanding general of the XXIV Panzer Corps on the Eastern Front. Then, in August he was given command of the XXXXVIII Panzer Corps. On 26 June 1944, *Generalleutnant* Gräser was awarded the 517th Oak Leaves for the taking of Aprilia. On 1 September 1944 he was promoted to *General der Panzertruppe* and named Commander-in-Chief of the 4th Panzer Army.

On 13 June 1944, after 30 days of close combat man against man, Gerhard Türke was decorated with the Close Combat Bar in Silver.

The battle for the European mainland went on. Allied troops advanced steadily and drove back the German defenders. Rome had been occupied by the Allies on 4 June. The British 8th Army had advanced to the Apennine positions. German forces took up position on the upper Arno and along the Tiber.

The defensive battle and subsequent fighting withdrawal on the Adriatic began in early July and lasted until the end of August. The first signs of a major attack did not appear until late August, after the Americans massed armored units for a drive through Florence in the direction of Futa Pass. On 5 September 1944, the German units moved in several stages into prepared positions, the "Emma Line."

Combat on German Soil

Positional warfare in the western Alps began on 23 September 1944. But German forces were not just facing collapse in southern Europe. In the west, too, there were clear signs of Germany's impending defeat. Allied forces had already reached the borders of the Reich.

The 3rd and 15th Panzer Divisions had already been withdrawn from Army Group Southwest in July 1944. *Generalfeldmarschall* Kesselring was not unaffected by the defeat in France, from where the victorious Allies had marched to the Reich frontier. The 3rd Division was rushed to Lorraine, where in August it began defensive fighting south of Verdun. The enemy pressure was too great, however, and the division withdrew through St, Mihiel toward Pont á Mousson. The end of September found it engaged in heavy fighting near Metz. The division was withdrawn and assembled in the Bedburg area. At the beginning of November, however, it received orders to attack the advancing Americans near Aachen. Since 5 October the Division had been under the command of *Generalmajor* Walter Denkert (1897-1982, Knight's Cross on 14 May 1944 as *Oberst* and acting commander of the 19th Panzer Division). The division's first assignment there was to widen the corridor to Aachen, first to the south (Verlautenheide) and then to the west (Ravelsburg). When this failed, it went over to the defensive near Würselen, north of Aachen. The third defensive battle at Aachen began on 23 November 1944.

In mid-November, Gerhard Türke received orders to defend the town of Röhe. His battalion was struck by the main enemy thrust, but managed to hold its position. The enemy attacked on the left and was beaten back by concentrated fire from the German infantry.

Türke's battalion, which had been ordered to support the 1st Battery of Flak Battalion 312, was able to repulse five attacks. Two tanks that made it to the church were knocked out by two of the battalion's drivers using magnetic mines.

In the evening the enemy fought his way into the southern part of the town. The 3rd Company of Panzer Battalion 103, which was deployed in that sector, supported a counterattack by the battalion and knocked out one enemy tank. Türke held on to the town for several days, even though his battalion, supported by *3./PzAbt. 103*, had been outflanked in the north and south. Then came the order to abandon the town at nightfall and fall back to a position at the eastern edge of the "Zukunft" coal mine, just south of the autobahn. Two assault guns of the 3rd Company of Panzer Battalion 103 were assigned to support the Türke Battalion.

The battalion manned trenches dug by the *Volkssturm*. These were more than man-deep, and after days of rain were full of water. Their walls were gradually collapsing. The battalion had to withstand the pressure resulting from the withdrawal of the Second Battalion in the direction of the city.

Soon afterwards the Americans began pounding the battalion's positions on the hill with artillery fire, and after about twenty minutes American infantry attacked. The first American troops entered the trench system and began taking prisoners. Then the grenadiers rose from cover and counterattacked. The communications trenches were placed under fire. The grenadiers fought the enemy infantry hand to hand. Each man was on his own, fighting for survival. When mud caused weapons to fail they used rifle butts. Meanwhile, the assault guns changed position and opened fire on the rear trenches.

The battalion's squads had rapidly gained ground, halted the American attack, and advanced deep into the system of trenches. After about half an hour roughly half the hill was back in German hands.

Hauptmann Türke assembled several grenadiers, and as quickly as possible attacked the Americans from the flank. They encountered heavy return fire. For the first time he grasped the scale of the American attack. After the few survivors surrendered, Türke realized that 30 grenadiers had been disarmed and captured.

The battle still raged in the sector where the assault guns were. Despite heavy casualties, Türke's men had succeeded in retaking most of the hill. American resistance gradually diminished.

The attack had been repulsed, and a total of 48 Americans taken prisoner. They had been forced to pay a heavy price in blood for their attempt to take Hill 154.4. The grenadiers once again occupied positions on the hill, but the Americans did not attack again. Thirty grenadiers who had been captured by the Americans were freed.

Toward evening the other battalions retired past the hill in good order and pulled back in the direction of Pützlohn. Türke and his men were ordered to abandon the hill. During the night German artillery shelled enemy concentrations in Pattern, Lohn, and Fronhoven, and the Türke Battalion was able to withdraw to Pützlohn under cover of darkness. After giving up the hill and the town, the division took up defensive positions in the Inde Position near Altdorf – Inden – Lammersdorf – Frenz.

On 26 November 1944, the 3rd Panzer Grenadier Division and its commander were mentioned in the *Wehrmacht* communiqué for the last time:

In the recent fighting near Aachen, the 3rd Panzer Grenadier Division under the command of *Generalmajor* Denkert and the 12th Volksgrenadier Division under *Generalmajor* Engel distinguished themselves through unshakable steadfastness and dogged resistance. Their exemplary conduct and perseverance was largely responsible for the failure of the enemy's attempt to break through in this sector.

The division was supposed to be relieved on the night of 28 November, but this could not be carried out due to intense enemy pressure. The enemy continued to press forward. The Türke Battalion, supported by the 2nd Company of Panzer Battalion 103, the 1st Company of Anti-Tank Battalion 3, and the 2nd Company of Armored Reconnaissance Battalion 103, occupied Lammersdorf. On 28 November, it fought off three more attacks supported by artillery and

Türke crawls from his regimental command post near Anzio.

fighter-bombers during the course of the day. After nightfall, the Americans entered several houses at the southern edge of the town and Türke ordered a counterattack. *Leutnant* Wild of the 2nd Company and *Leutnant* Schramm of 2nd Company, Armored Reconnaissance Battalion, carried out the attack with five NCOs and enlisted men, plus two assault guns and three tank destroyers. They cleared the town and took 18 prisoners. The enemy's attempt to enter the town had failed.

Meanwhile, in the Aachen area, the division had also had to fight off three American attacks with powerful air and artillery support. A delaying action made it possible for the division to fall back to prepared positions on the Inde River on either side of Inden.

The division withdrew into the Bedburg area to rest and reequip. After eight days, at the beginning of December orders came for it to move into the Zülpich area, closer to its new operational area. The buildup for the Ardennes offensive had begun.

Battle Group Türke was formed on 4 December. It consisted of the regiment's I Battalion, four assault guns of the 3rd Company, Panzer Battalion 103, and six tank destroyers and three anti-tank guns of Anti-Tank Battalion 3. The 227th Volksgrenadier Division was designated as reserve. Moved to the area west of Nideggen, Türke was supposed to support a counterattack towards the Burgberg east of Bergstein. Preparations were made, but then the operation was called off. Battle Group Türke was released to rejoin the division.

Knight's Cross Winners of the 29th Motorized Infantry-Grenadier Regiment of the 3rd Motorized Infantry Division / 3rd Panzer Grenadier Division

Name	Rank/Position	Date	Reason	Fate
von Beaulieu-Marconnay Baron Sigurd-Horstmar	*Oberst* and C.O. Gren.-Rgt. 29 (mot.)	20/1/1943	Battle of Stalingrad	Died as a prisoner of the Soviets in the Krasnopolye-Gondorovka POW camp
Borchert, Ernst	*Oberleutnant* and C.O. 1./Inf.-Rgt. 29 (mot.)	29/9/1941	For the taking of the Lovaty bridge near Lipno	Killed on 1/5/1945 as *Major* and operations officer of the 3rd Parachute Division near Drolshagen, Sauerland
Gräser, Fritz-Hubert 517th Oak Leaves	*Oberst* and C.O. of Inf.-Rgt. 29 (mot.) *Generalleutnant*, C.O. 3rd Panzer Grenadier Division	19/7/1940 26/6/1944	For the crossing of the Aisne For the taking of Aprilia	Died 4/10/1960 in Göttingen
Jetting, Ernst	*Oberfeldwebel* and platoon leader 1./Gren.Rgt. 29 (mot.)	4/6/1944	For holding Monte Corno	Died 24/12/1999 in Augsburg
Kracht, Hermann	*Oberfeldwebel* and platoon leader 12(MG)./Gren.Rgt. 29 (mot.)	25/12/1944 (posthum.)	For the attack on the Aprilia cemetery	KIA on 2/6/1944 east of Aprilia, Italy
Schlömer, Helmuth 161st Oak Leaves	*Oberst* and C.O. 5th Rifle Regiment *Generalmajor* and C.O. 3. Inf.Div. (mot.)	2/10/1941 23/12/1943	For the fighting at Leningrad For the fighting at Stalingrad	Died on 18/8/1995 in Minden
Semrau, Norbert	*Leutnant* d.R. and platoon leader 1./Gren.Rgt. 29 (mot.)	6/4/1944	For holding the hill north of Aprilia	Died 29/9/2003 in Lüneburg
Türke, Gerhard	*Oberleutnant* d.R. and C.O. 3./Gren.Rgt. 29 (mot.)	17/12/1942	For the defense of Hill 135.1 at Marinovka near Stalingrad	Died 21/11/1999 in Gelsenkirchen, North Rhine-Westphalia
Walter, Gerhard	*Oberfeldwebel* and platoon leader 5.(MG)./Gren.Rgt. 29 (mot.)	1/1/1944	For the counterattack at Monte Corno	KIA in Italy on 30/1/1944

Promotion to *Major* and the German Cross in Gold

Gerhard Türke was promoted to the rank of *Major* with an effective date of 1 November 1944, and was taken into the active officer corps. On 22 December 1944, he was awarded the German Cross in Gold in recognition of the success of the 4th (Machine-Gun) Company of the 29th Motorized Grenadier Regiment and his command of I Battalion, 29th Motorized Grenadier Regiment.

When the Ardennes Offensive began in January 1945, the division, which had been transferred to the south on 17 December 1944, was west of Bastogne. It was supposed to bar the roads leading to Bastogne to the southwest near Sibret and Assenois. When it was unable to achieve its objective it conducted a fighting withdrawal to the south and west, during which it was engaged in costly fighting and badly decimated.

There was now no hope of avoiding defeat, as the Allies drove into the heart of the Reich. For the division and the 29th Motorized Grenadier Regiment, the retreat began in February 1945. They fell back through Gmünd and Mechernich to the southern outskirts of Cologne. In March the division crossed the Rhine near Rodenkirchen. In mid-March the Pioneer Battalion was attached to the Türke Battalion, as its companies were down to ten to twelve men. During the fighting near Oberpleiß the pioneers, fighting as infantry and organized into a weak company, suffered heavy casualties.

The End of the War and Capture

The fighting in the Ruhr Pocket began on 25 March 1945. The units of the 3rd Panzer Grenadier Division withdrew through Sieg, Schmallenberg, and Winterberg to Lüdenscheid. On 2 April they attacked towards Medebach, took the town, and blocked an American advance road to the north. An attempt to continue the fighting failed, however. The division was burnt out. Most of its tanks and guns had been blown up after running out of fuel. There were no more supplies. The division's last action took place in the Plattenberg area. The remnants of the division moved through Altena east of the eastern Iserlohn pocket to Östrich, west of the city. After *General* Beyerlein surrendered Iserlohn to the Americans – and with it the pocket – on 16 April 1945, Gerhard Türke was taken prisoner. By that point his battalion, like the others, was down to just 75 men.

The war was over. Iserlohn was the only city in the big Ruhr Pocket that was "honorably surrendered" to the enemy. Research later confirmed that it was the only city in which this happened. After several attempts Gerhard Türke managed to escape, demonstrating the same will to survive and maintain his freedom that he had shown at Hill 135.1 near Marinovka.

He found a new home, first in Lower Saxony and later in North Rhine-Westphalia. He later resumed his career as a teacher and died in Gelsenkirchen on 21 November 1991.

Retired *Major* Gerhard Türke died in Gelsenkirchen on 21/11/1991.

Sources:

Ralf Schumann Archive
Private possessions and estate of Retired Major Gerhard Türke

Photos:

Ralf Schumann Archive
Estate of Retired Major Gerhard Türke (+)

Text and Research:

Ralf Schumann

Acknowledgments:

The author wishes to thank Retired Major Gerhard Türke (+), who spoke about his military experiences in personal conversations with the author, and his lovely wife, who after his death granted access to his files, documents, and photos, making the writing of this publication possible. I am also grateful to Manfred Franzke of UNITEC Media Sales and Distribution, who by publishing this documentation made it available to a wide circle of readers, and to his wife and two sons, who gave up their valuable spare time with their father so that this book could be completed.

Heinrich "Heinz" Bär

Top Jet Fighter Ace with 16 Victories

BY RALF SCHUMANN

Foreword

If one examines the list of the most successful German fighters pilots of the WWII, in eighth place one finds the name Heinz Bär, with 221 confirmed victories. This is 5.5 times as many victories as scored by the leading American ace, Major Richard J. Bong. What is remarkable, however, is the fact that Bär also scored 16 confirmed victories while flying the Messerschmitt Me 262, the first operational jet fighter, making him the top-scoring jet pilot of all time, and that he achieved this feat at a time when air superiority over Germany had long since been conceded to the Allies.

Together with a handful of other aces in Jagdverband 44, Bär laid the groundwork which positively influenced the coming generations of jet fighter pilots.

Heinz Bär was a fighter pilot with special qualities. He distinguished himself in every theater of WWII, whether against the overwhelming numbers of the western Allies, in the vastness of Russia, or in the Mediterranean theater or the fierce heat of North Africa. With 125 victories, after Hans-Joachim Marseille (1919-1942) he was the most successful fighter pilot against the western Allies.

He especially stood out as a day-fighter pilot in the Defense of the Reich, repeatedly demonstrating bravado and dauntlessness in tough air battles and also becoming the leading scorer among jet pilots. He also did not hold back against his commander-in-chief, refusing to accept his unwarranted criticism, which resulted in Göring demoting him from *Gruppenkommandeur* to *Staffelkapitän*.

All the more tragic was his premature death in 1957 in the crash of a sporting aircraft.

Ralf Schumann

Decorations:

	Long Service Decoration 4th Class
	Iron Cross, Second Class
	Iron Cross, First Class
	Operational Flying Clasp for Fighter Pilots in Gold
	Knight's Cross of the Iron Cross
	31st Knight's Cross of the Iron Cross with Oak Leaves
	Wound Badge in Black
	7th Knight's Cross with Oak Leaves and Swords
	Honor Goblet for Distinguished Achievement in the Air War
	German Cross in Gold
23/08/1943	Winter Battle in the East Medal (Ostmedaille)
plus:	Memorial Medal for 01/10/1938 (Sudetenland)
	Medal for the German-Italian Campaign in Africa
	Operational Flying Clasp for Fighter Pilots in Gold with "1000" Pendant

Promotions:

Gefreiter	
Obergefreiter	
Unteroffizier	
Feldwebel	
named officer candidate	
Leutnant	(wartime officer, seniority date 01/05/1940)
Oberleutnant	(wartime officer, seniority date 01/08/1941)
Hauptmann	(wartime officer, promoted by Reichsmarschall)
Major	(wartime officer, seniority date 01/09/1943)
Oberstleutnant	

Combat Missions:

More than 1,000 combat missions on the Eastern and Western Fronts, in the Mediterranean Theater and Africa

Victories:

221 (16 on the Me 262) confirmed victories
(96 in the east and 125 in the west, including 21 heavy bombers and 1 Mosquito and 65 in the Mediterranean Theater, 22 of them in North Africa)

Command Positions:

20/07/1941 to 11/05/1942	Staffelkapitän of 12. Staffel, Jagdgeschwader 51
11/05/1942 to 06/08/1943	Kommandeur of I. Gruppe, Jagdgeschwader 77
15/02/1944 to 11/05/1944	Kommandeur of II. Gruppe, Jagdgeschwader 1
11/05/1944 to 20/05/1944	Kommodore of Jagdgeschwader 1 "Oesau"
01/06/1944 to 13/02/1945	Kommodore of Jagdgeschwader 3 "Udet"
14/02/1945 to 25/04/1945	Kommandeur of Ergänzungsgruppe 2
26/04/1945 to 03/05/1945	Kommandeur of Jagdverband 44

Operational Aircraft Types Flown:

Messerschmitt Bf 109 E, F, G, Focke-Wulf Fw 190 A-7, A-8, Messerschmitt Me 262 A-1a

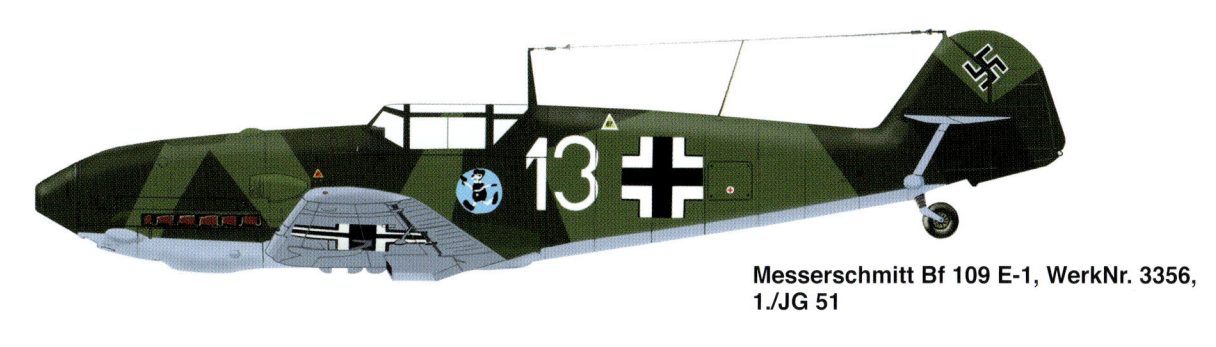

VOLUME 2   Heinrich "Heinz" Bär Profile

Messerschmitt Bf 109 E-1, WerkNr. 3356,
1./JG 51

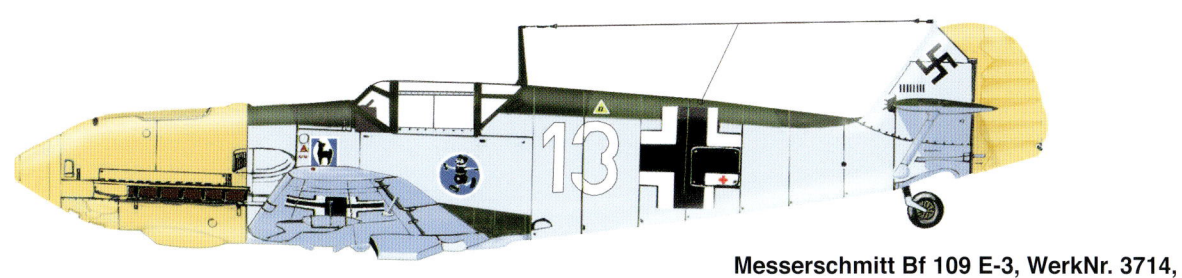

Messerschmitt Bf 109 E-3, WerkNr. 3714,
I./JG 51

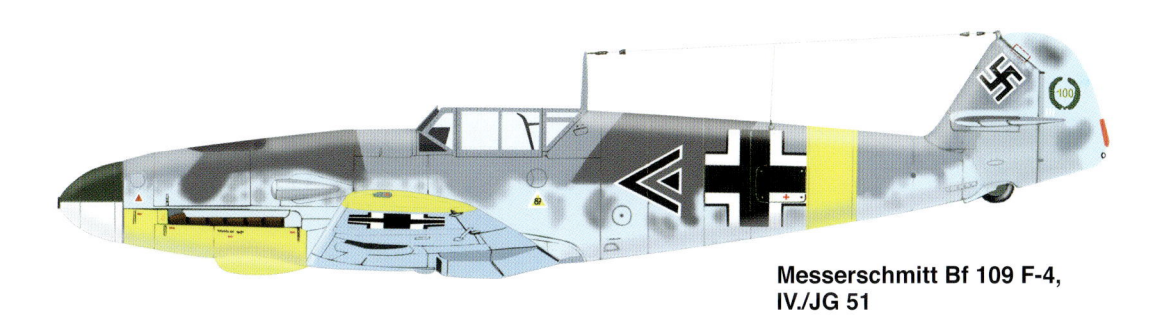

Messerschmitt Bf 109 F-4,
IV./JG 51

Focke-Wulf Fw 190 A-8, WerkNr. 431007,
II./JG 1

Messerschmitt Me 262 A-1a, WerkNr.
110559, JV 44

55

School Days and Training

Oskar Heinrich "Heinz" Bär came into the world in Sommerfeld, near Leipzig in Saxony, on 25 March 1913 as the son of a farmer. Interested in aviation from an early age, there was never any question that he would become a pilot. In 1928, at the age of 15, he joined a gliding club in his Saxon homeland. After completing school he learned about farming and began training to become an agricultural official. His career of choice, however, was to become a pilot with the airline *Lufthansa*.

Financial difficulties in the depression years robbed him of the opportunity to train as a civilian pilot, however. Thus, in 1933 he volunteered for service in the *Reichswehr*, and on 4 April 1934 he joined the 3rd Motor Transport Company in Leipzig, having signed up for a twelve-year service commitment. Following promotion to *Gefreiter* on 4 April 1935, that summer Bär was transferred to the Luftwaffe. Contrary to his wishes, however, he was not assigned to a fighter unit, but instead was attached to the airfield operating company of a bomber wing, where he performed general duties until 31 October 1937. His efforts to become an airman finally bore fruit. From 1 November 1937 to 31 March 1938 he trained at the flight training school in Oldenburg, after which he was transferred to the school in Hildesheim. On 16 May 1938, Bär received his C II certificate at the flight training school in Ludwigslust. Then, from 7 July to 14 August 1939, he was assigned to the instrument flight school in Neuburg an der Donau. On 1 September 1939, Bär was attached to the *I. Gruppe* of *Jagdgeschwader 135*, but as an *Unteroffizier* and qualified transport pilot he was placed in charge of the Ju 52 operated by the *Gruppenstab* instead of becoming a fighter pilot. This *Gruppe* later became the *I. Gruppe* of *Jagdgeschwader 233*, and ultimately of *Jagdgeschwader 51*. Then Bär was assigned to the *1. Staffel* as a fighter pilot. His *Staffelkapitän* was *Oberleutnant* Douglas Pitcairn. Pitcairn was an experienced pilot with war experience. During the Spanish Civil War he had led the *3. Staffel* of J/88 – part of the "Legion Condor" – preceding Adolf Galland (1912-1996). Pitcairn led his *Staffel*, which was equipped with the He 51, and operated as a close-support unit with success from April to 26 July 1937. Following the end of the civil war and the Legion Condor's return to Germany, in 1939 Pitcairn was awarded the Spanish Cross in Gold with Swords. In August 1940, he was transferred to the flight training school in Magdeburg, and in 1942 was promoted to *Major im Generalstab*. He had commanded the *Staffel* in which Bär now served since returning from Spain. Over time, he unofficially trained him how to fly fighter aircraft.

Sommerfeld, the birthplace of Heinz Bär.

***Oberleutnant* Douglas Pitcairn, *Staffelkapitän* of 1./JG 51 and Bär's superior. He trained him on fighter aircraft and also grounded him for two weeks.**

25 September 1939. The Bf 109 E-1, *Werknummer* 3356, flown by *Unteroffizier* Heinz Bär as a member of 1./JG 51 in Speyer.

The Outbreak of War and First Success

When war broke out on 1 September 1939, Bär, called "Pritzl" by his friends, was a pilot in the *1. Staffel* of *Jagdgeschwader 51*. Heinz Bär was now flying a Messerschmitt Bf 109 E-3 with the aircraft number "White 13." The *Geschwader* was commanded by *Oberst* Theo Osterkamp (1892-1975), a fighter ace in WWI with 32 victories and a wearer of the *Pour le Mérite*. Bär scored his first and the *Geschwader*'s second victory on 25 September 1939, shooting down a French Curtiss P-36 over the German border. For this he was awarded the Iron Cross, Second Class on 29 September.

In the period from 26 August 1939 to 27 March 1940, Bär completed 52 combat missions, defensive sorties over Germany's western frontier. He flew one more by 9 May 1940.

Bär, whose special attributes had earned the notice of his superiors, was grounded for two weeks by *Staffelkapitän Hauptmann* Pitcairn in May 1940. During a ground attack sortie on 30 April he failed to abide by mission orders, flying too low and exceeding the specified number of firing passes, and as a result his aircraft was damaged. It was a tough lesson.

During the early days of the campaign in the west, however, over Holland Bär added two more missions to his total. When the German army broke through to the English Channel and faced the French Army on the First World War battlefields of Flanders, Bär flew another 33 sorties in 23 days. On 3 June he and his *Geschwader* took part in a major raid on French airfields in the Paris area, attacking the French air force and its ground organization, as well as transportation targets. By 12 July he added another 25 combat missions over the Somme, Dunkirk, defending the German Bight, and over the Dutch coast. During the fighting in France he increased his victory total to eight. His total included four French and four British machines.

At the beginning of his career as a fighter pilot. *Feldwebel* **Heinz Bär in his aircraft "White 13," a dark-green Bf 109 E-1.** *Staffelkapitän* **Douglas Pitcairn brought 3.J/88's Mickey Mouse emblem back with him from Spain.**

On 29/9/1939 Heinz Bär was decorated with the Iron Cross, Second Class.

The Battle of Britain

On 13 July 1940, the Luftwaffe launched its aerial campaign against the British air force and its ground organization, the aircraft industry, and major seaports in England.

Since 23 July 1940, *Jagdgeschwader 51* had been under the command of *Major* Werner Mölders (1913-1941). He was to become the great role model for many fighter pilots and synonymous with chivalry. Lovingly called "Daddy" by his men, it was Mölders who first reached the magical 100 victory mark. In recognition of this, on 15 July 1941 Mölders became the first soldier and fighter pilot to receive the Knight's Cross with Oak Leaves and Diamonds. In his honor the *Geschwader* was awarded the title "*Jagdgeschwader Mölders.*" On 1 August 1940 Bär, who had been an officer candidate since 1 June, was promoted to *Leutnant* for bravery in the face of the enemy.

Heinz Bär scored 17 victories during the so-called Battle of Britain. On 2 September 1940 he was himself shot down over the Channel. He was forced to bale out and was picked up by the air-sea rescue service. Bär's mission total rose steadily, and he added another 16 sorties by 6 September. Fighter sweeps were not the only duty of the fighter pilots, however. They also flew escort for bomber units, conducted defensive patrols over the Channel Coast, attacked RAF airfields, and supported attacks against the enemy's aviation industry. As a result Bär's mission total grew daily. By 23 May 1941 his total had risen by 56 more, and by the time his unit was transferred to the Eastern Front he had shot down 22 enemy aircraft. Since 24 May 1941 he had worn the Operational Flying Clasp for Fighter Pilots in Gold.

Theo Osterkamp. He led JG 51 from 19/9/1939 to 23/7/1940 and was Bär's first *Kommodore*. He was awarded the Knight's Cross on 22/8/1940.

Pihen, France, 2 September 1940. The tail of Bär's Bf 109 with eight victory bars.

Werner Mölders, here as an *Oberstleutnant* (1913-1941), succeeded Osterkamp as commander of *Jagdgeschwader* 51. On 15/7/1941 he became the first fighter pilot to reach the 100 victory mark, and the same day became the first German soldier to be awarded the Knight's Cross with Oak Leaves, Swords, and Diamonds. After his death in a crash in November 1941 the *Geschwader* was awarded the honorary title "Jagdgeschwader Mölders." He scored a total of 115 victories, 68 of them in the west.

A *Staffel* of *I. Gruppe* of *Jagdgeschwader* 51 before taking off on a mission during the Battle of Britain.

In the west, 1940. Heinz Bär at the beginning of his stellar career as a fighter pilot.

On 6/7/1940 Bär was awarded the Iron Cross, First Class, and on 1/8/1940 was promoted to *Leutnant*.

A Bf 109 E-1 of *8. Staffel* of JG 51 at the start of the western campaign.

Spitfire fighters of the Royal Air Force over France.

Rearming a Bf 109 E-1 of 8./JG 51.

Successful German fighter pilots during the Battle of Britain. From left: *Oberstleutnant*e Adolf Galland, Günther Lützow, Werner Mölders, and Günther Baron von Maltzahn. In the center is *Generalmajor* Theo Osterkamp, at that time *Jagdfliegerführer* 2 on the Channel Coast.

Servicing and aligning the guns of a Bf 109 E-1.

On 25/5/1942 Bär was awarded the Operational Flying Clasp for Fighter Pilots in Gold.

Coquelle, France, 21 April 1941: 15 victory bars on the tail of Bär's Bf 109 E.

Action over Russia

Following the German invasion of the Soviet Union on 22 June 1941, Bär steadily increased both his combat mission and victory totals. It began with support for army units during the crossing of the Bug River, the Battle of Bialystok, and the breaching of the Stalin Line. Bär flew another 48 combat missions by 20 July 1941, shooting down five bombers—victories 23 to 27—on 30 June. On 2 July 1941, he was awarded the Knight's Cross after his 29th victory. On 20 July, Bär was transferred to the *IV. Gruppe* and took over as commander of the *12. Staffel*, replacing Karl-Gottfried Nordmann (1915-1982), who had been appointed *Gruppenkommandeur*. At that time he flew the Messerschmitt Bf 109 F.

After *Oberst* Mölders was named *General der Jagdflieger*, on 21 July 1941 *Major im Generalstab* Friedrich Beckh (1908-1942) assumed command of *Jagdgeschwader 51*. He would be awarded the Knight's Cross on 18 September 1941 after 27 victories. Heinz Bär continued flying missions over the Eastern Front, and by the end of January 1942 he had entered 400 combat missions and 120 patrol flights in his logbook.

On 14 August 1941, Heinz Bär was promoted to *Oberleutnant* with a seniority date of 1 August 1941, and on the same day, 43 days after he had received the Knight's Cross, he became the 31st member of the armed forces and 12th fighter pilot to be awarded the Knight's Cross with Oak Leaves.

When the attack on the Soviet Union began on 22 June 1941, *I.*, *II.*, and *III. Gruppe* of JG 51 were concentrated on airfields near the border. *IV. Gruppe* was initially attached to JG 53.

The Knight's Cross of the Iron Cross.

On 2/7/1941 Heinz Bär was awarded the Knight's Cross after his 29th victory. On 20/7/1941, early in the Russian campaign, he took over as *Staffelkapitän* of 12./JG 41, and on 14/8/1941 was promoted to *Oberleutnant*.

Three successful pilots of IV./JG 51. From left: *Oberfeldwebel* Heinrich Hoffmann (Knight's Cross on 12/8/1941), *Oberleutnant* Gottfried Nordmann, and Heinz Bär, *Staffelkapitän* of 12./JG 51 in Russia.

Kommodore Oberst Mölders congratulates Bär on the awarding of the Knight's Cross. On the right is *Leutnant* Erwin Fleig (1912-1986), a frequent wing man and witness of Mölders. Fleig was awarded the Knight's Cross on 12/8/1941 after 26 victories.

Whilst the panzers under *General* Guderian (1888-1954) were driving towards the southeast—with the goal of linking up with Army Group South east of Kiev—*Jagdgeschwader 51* flew interception missions against Soviet aircraft attempting to attack the German spearheads and also strafed enemy airfields. During one such mission on 31 August 1941, after his 80th victory *Oberleutnant* Bär was shot down over enemy territory and obliged to make a forced landing. He sprained both ankles in the crash-landing and every step caused him terrible pain. Nevertheless, he got away from his machine as quickly as he could, expecting Russian search parties to appear at any moment. He hid in bushes until the next morning and then set off towards the northwest in the

Star Bykhov, Eastern Front, 15 July 1941: the tail of *Kommodore* Werner Mölders' Bf 109 F with 101 victory bars.

Bär with comrades after a mission over Russia. On the left is then *Leutnant* Herbert Huppertz (1919-1944), who was awarded the Knight's Cross on 30/8/1941. He was awarded the 512th Oak Leaves posthumously with the rank of *Major* on 24/6/1944.

On 14/8/1941, Bär became the 31st member of the armed services and 12th fighter pilot to be awarded the Oak Leaves following his 62nd victory. He was simultaneously promoted to *Oberleutnant*.

The Knight's Cross with Oak Leaves.

Bär was awarded the Wound Badge in Black on 26/11/1941.

direction of the German lines. Before starting he had hidden his decorations in his pants pockets, together with his watch and pistol. He combed his hair over his face, turned his flight jacket inside out and stuffed it with straw, and threw away his flying boots. Thus disguised as a Russian peasant, after walking for two days and nights he reached the German lines. Completely exhausted, after returning to his *Geschwader* he spent two months in hospital. In his absence *Leutnant* Bernd Gallowitsch (1918-1993), who was awarded the Knight's Cross on 24 January 1942, led his *Staffel*.

On 1 September 1941 Bär was promoted to *Hauptmann*. The promotion was ordered by *Reichsmarschall* Göring himself after hearing about Bär's downing, flight, and return. On 26 November 1941 Bär was awarded the Wound Badge in Silver.

On returning to his unit, he again took command of his *Staffel* and also led the *Stabsschwarm* (staff flight) in place of the *Kommodore*, who was unfit to fly. On 12 February 1942 Bär scored his 90th victory, and four days later he became the seventh recipient of the Knight's Cross with Oak Leaves and Swords. He was the fifth fighter pilot and member of the Luftwaffe to receive the decoration and the second in the *Geschwader* after Mölders.

Receiving the prestigious decoration was no reason for him to take it easy on himself. On 1 May 1942 he took over the *I. Gruppe* of *Jagdgeschwader 77*. He scored his 100th victory on 19 May 1942, and on 1 June was awarded the Honor Goblet for Distinguished Achievement in the Air War, a decoration normally awarded before the Knight's Cross. Because of his rapid success, however, he was already one of the Luftwaffe's leading aces. In the period from 1 May to 28 June 1942 he led the *Gruppe* in missions against the Soviet air force during the breakthrough battle on the Kerch Peninsula and the drive on Sevastopol. On 27 June he was awarded the German Cross in Gold.

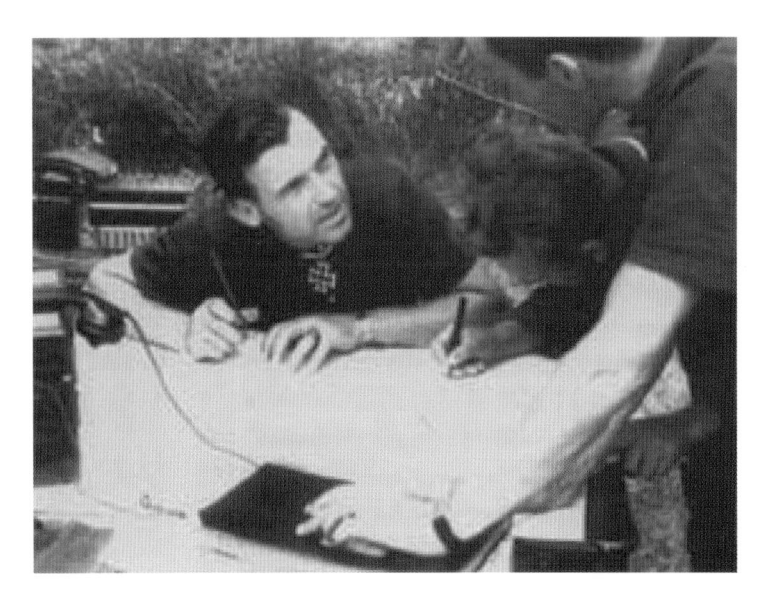

Bär as *Staffelkapitän* of 12./JG 51 in Russia while writing operations reports after a combat mission.

Heinz Bär and *Oberfeldwebel* Heinrich Hoffmann (1913-1941) of Bär's *12. Staffel* of JG 51 at the beginning of the Russian campaign. Hoffmann was awarded the Knight's Cross on 12/08/1941. He was posted missing near Shatalovka on 03/10/1941, and was awarded the 36th Oak Leaves posthumously on 19/10/1941. Hoffmann had 63 victories when he went missing. He was the first non-commissioned officer in the *Wehrmacht* to receive this honor.

Bär, Werner Baumbach, and Hermann Graf receive the Swords from Adolf Hitler in Führer Headquarters.

After his 90th victory, on 16 February 1942 Bär became the 7th member of the armed services and the 5th fighter pilot to be awarded the Knight's Cross with Oak Leaves and Swords.

The Oak Leaves with Swords.

To mark the National-Socialist Flying Corps' seventh anniversary, a ceremony was held at the corps' training building in Berlin that was attended by past and current members. In the photo, from left to right, are: *NSFK-Obergruppenführer* Sauke representing the corps commander of the National-Socialist Flying Corps, an unidentified member of the corps, *NSFK-Oberführer* and *Hauptmann* Bär, *NSFK-Obergruppenführer* and *Oberstleutnant* d.R. Harry von Bülow-Bothkamp (Knight's Cross on 22/8/1940), *Oberleutnant* Werner Thierfelder (Knight's Cross on 10/10/1941) and, partly hidden, *Oberfeldwebel* Walter Ohlrogge (Knight's Cross on 4/11/1941).

April 1942. The Bf 109 F flown by Bär as *Kommandeur* of IV./JG 51.

The same machine after Bär's crash landing.

In May 1942 Bär left his old *Geschwader* to become *Kommandeur* of *I. Gruppe* of JG 77.

Bär in conversation with Karl-Gottfried Nordmann. Bär took over Nordmann's *12. Staffel* and Nordmann became *Kommandeur* of *I. Gruppe*.

Karl-Gottfried Nordmann's camouflaged aircraft at Shatalovka, Russia.

Bär scored victory number 100 on 19 May 1942.

Kerch, the Eastern Front, 19 May 1942: Bär, *Kommandeur* of IV./JG 51, beside the tail of his Bf 109 F with markings representing 103 victories.

22 May 1942: Bär with other successful pilots of I./JG 51. From left to right: Obfw. Heinrich Höfemeier (51 victories), Lt. Erwin Fleig (65 victories), Hptm. Bär, and Hptm. Heinrich Krafft (48 victories). The four fighter pilots had more than 250 victories between them when this photo was taken.

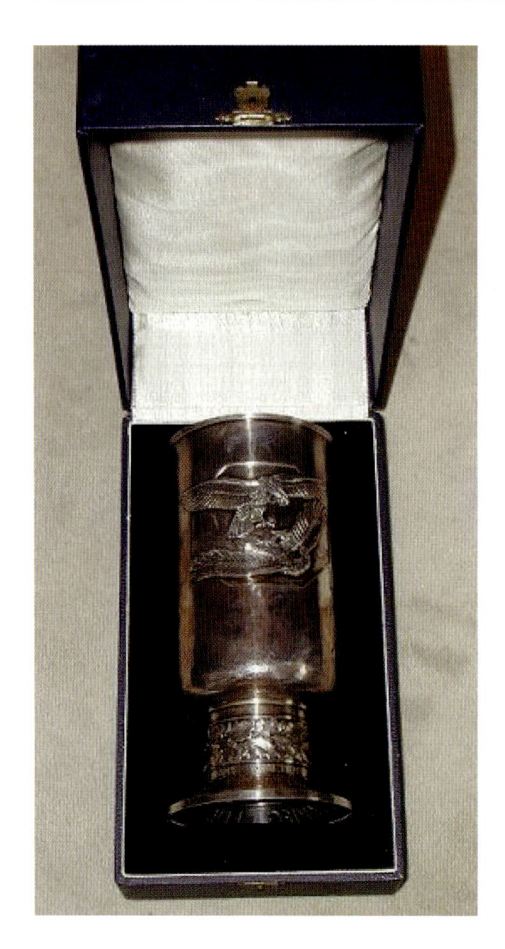

Bär was awarded the Luftwaffe Honor Goblet on 01/06/1942.

The tail of Bär's Bf 109 with markings for 113 victories, photographed on the Kerch Peninsula on 27 June 1942.

He was awarded the German Cross in Gold on the same day.

Action in the Mediterranean Theater and over North Africa

Following the transfer of *Jagdgeschwader 77* under *Major* Joachim Müncheberg (1918-1943) to the Mediterranean, from 5 July to 25 October 1942 Bär flew missions from Sicily against British bases on the island of Malta, shooting down four enemy aircraft.

The German air staff had meanwhile developed plans to relieve the exhausted *Jagdgruppen* based in North Africa. The first to leave was the *III. Gruppe* of *Jagdgeschwader 53*, which left North Africa and moved to Sicily. Bär's *Gruppe* arrived to take its place on 27 October 1942. Two of the unit's *Staffelkapitäne* were also leading aces: *Hauptmann* Friedrich Geißhardt (1919-1943), a wearer of the Oak Leaves with 91 victories, and *Oberleutnant* Siegfried Freytag (1919-2003), a wearer of the Knight's Cross with 70 victories to his credit. Other members of the *Gruppe* included *Leutnant* Heinz-Edgar Berres (1920-1943), the *Gruppe* adjutant, who would be awarded the Knight's Cross posthumously on 19 September 1943 for 52 victories; and *Leutnant* Armin Köhler (1912-1999), who ended the war as a *Major* and *Kommandeur* of III./JG 77 and also received the Knight's Cross after 40 victories. The *Geschwader* arrived without ground personnel, and for weeks was looked after by *Jagdgeschwader 27*. Now led by Bär, the *Gruppe* had amassed more than 750 victories. However, the initial optimism soon disappeared when the men found themselves facing a hopeless situation.

The *Geschwaderstab*, under *Major* Müncheberg, was supposed to arrive in North Africa the next day. Müncheberg had desert experience from his days as *Staffelkapitän* of 7./JG 26.

Heinz Bär was also to become one of the best fighter pilots in the North African theater. On 30 October Bär's *Gruppe* conducted a fighter sweep, during which he and *Oberleutnant* Freytag shot down two British Curtiss fighters near El Alamein. Bär continued his successful streak on 1 November, shooting down another enemy aircraft. The next fell on 3 November. A Kittyhawk of 450 Squadron followed on 9 November. On 3 November the *I. Gruppe* scored a total of seven victories, including five by *Hauptmann* Bär. He shot down his first two victims, probably aircraft of 127 Squadron, at about noon. The other three he shot down within the space of 15 minutes in the late afternoon. On the morning of 11 November there were numerous large combats over the German fighters fields, in the course of which Bär's *Gruppe* claimed eleven victories against a force of 50 P-40s and ten Airacobras. Bär himself claimed two more enemy aircraft that day. Then the *Gruppe* moved again, first to Martuba, and then two days later to Benghazi.

Heinz Bär was promoted to *Major* on 1/3/1943.

Spring 1943: "Pritzl" Bär, *Kommandeur* of I./JG 77, with pilots of his *Gruppe*, Fatnassa airfield in Tunisia. On the left is *Leutnant* Armin Köhler, who later won the Knight's Cross.

Major Joachim Müncheberg (1918-1943), *Kommodore* of JG 77, which he led in North Africa and the Mediterranean Theater.

In Tunisia, waiting for what was to come ...

Müncheberg was awarded the Knight's Cross on 14/9/1940, the 12th Oak Leaves on 7/5/1941, and the 19th Swords on 9/9/1942.

On 7 December 1942, two Spitfires of 601 Squadron fell to Bär's guns. The following day he claimed three more victories, increasing his victory total to 136 confirmed. On 11 December he shot down a Curtiss for the 800th victory of the *I. Gruppe* of *Jagdgeschwader 77*.

On 14 December Bär claimed two victories, raising his total since arriving in Africa to 22. On 16 December the *Gruppe* moved to Arco Philaenorum, where it remained for a month.

On 25 January 1943, Bär's *Gruppe* became involved in a combat with 20 enemy fighters, during which he claimed his 148th and 149th victories. Three days later he claimed three more victories, and on 4 February shot down a B-17.

1 March 1943 found the *Gruppe* stationed in Fatnassa, Tunisia, flying the Bf 109 G-6. On that day Bär was promoted to *Major*. By then he had achieved 164 victories. In the course of the day he added one more victory and also damaged a Spitfire. Altogether Bär shot down 39 enemy aircraft over Tunisia. Then the *Geschwader* was dealt a heavy blow, when *Major* Müncheberg was killed after his Messerschmitt lost a wing during a dog fight.

On 7 May the *Geschwader* was ordered back from Africa. *Jagdgeschwader 77*'s part in the war in Africa was over. It had shot down a total of 333 enemy aircraft. Bär's *Gruppe* claimed a total of 140 victories over Africa, of which 61 were credited to him.

Following the *Geschwader*'s withdrawal from North Africa, Bär was ordered to Karinhall to report to *Reichsmarschall* Göring (1893-1946). Only three months after his promotion to *Major* his career was about to come to an abrupt halt.

Göring went after Bär using every nasty trick, indirectly calling him a coward. All of the accusations made by Göring were unfounded. Because Bär refused to allow himself to be called down without responding, Göring accused him of insubordination and dereliction of duty. This most probably cost him the Diamonds. Bär also did not receive the Pilot's Badge with Diamonds from the Luftwaffe commander-in-chief as his comrades expected. Instead he was relieved as *Gruppenkommandeur*, demoted to *Staffelkapitän,* and transferred to a fighter replacement training *Gruppe* in the south of France. Bär accepted the demotion, drove back to the airfield, and said nothing of the incident.

Tunisia: a *Staffel* painter applies a fresh victory bar to the rudder of Müncheberg's aircraft.

Heinz Bär was awarded the East Medal on 23/08/1943.

Bär and Armin Köhler (left), also an ace with JG 77 in Africa.

From left: Friedrich Geißhardt (1919-1943), I./JG 77, Günther Baron von Maltzahn (1910-1953), *Kommodore* of JG 53 "Pik-As," and Heinz Bär at the beginning of 1943 in Tunisia in front of a Bf 109 G during servicing. *Jagdgeschwader* 53 and 77 relieved JG 27 in North Africa.

"Pritzl" Bär watches aircraft of JG 77 returning from a mission in Tunisia.

The tough fighting over the North African theater also left its scars on the face of Heinz Bär.

Major Bär in conversation with *Kommodore* Müncheberg. In the center is Lt. Armin Köhler, final rank *Hauptmann* (1912-1999, Knight's Cross on 7/2/1945).

Müncheberg was killed on 23/3/1943 southwest of Maknassy, in Tunisia, while on his 500th combat mission.

Bär and *Generalfeldmarschall* Hugo Sperrle.

For his actions over the North African theater, Bär was also awarded the Medal for the German-Italian Campaign in Africa.

Hans-Joachim Marseille (1919-1942), the "Star of Africa." Only he shot down more western opponents than Heinz Bär. He claimed a total of 158 enemy aircraft (151 over Africa).

Führer Headquarters, 20 January 1944: at about 11:00 Hitler personally presented the "Swords portfolio" to officers of the Luftwaffe: Bär, Baumbach, Druschel, Gollob, Galland, Helbig, Graf, Ihlefeld, Lent, Lützow, Oesau, Nowotny, Peltz, and Wilke. He also presented the award individually to Lüth, Rommel, Rudel, and Suhren. After Müncheberg's "hero's death," the Swords portfolio was sent to his family. This was the only known presentation of the Swords portfolio.

In March 1944, Bär was tasked with the duties of the *Geschwaderkommodore* of JG 1, and on 12 May he was named *Kommodore* for eight days after the death of *Oberst* Walter Oesau (3rd winner of the Swords). He had previously commanded the unit's *II. Gruppe*. This photo was taken after Bär's promotion to *Major* by the *Reichsmarschall* on 1/9/1942.

Oberst Walter Oesau (1913-1944) was shot down and killed near St. Vith in Belgium on 11 May 1944. At the time of his death he had 127 victories. His unit, *Jagdgeschwader* 1, was awarded the honorary title "Jagdgeschwader Oesau."

Kommodore Heinz Bär (right) briefs his pilots of *Jagdgeschwader* 1 prior to an operation.

22 April 1944 in Strömede. The tail of Heinz Bär's Fw 190 A-7 (*Werknummer* 431007) with markings representing 200 victories over aircraft of four countries. This was the aircraft he flew as a "*Staffel* leader" in II./JG 1.

Major Heinz Bär's "Red 13," a Focke-Wulf Fw 190 A-8 of II./JG 1 in Strömede on 25 April 1944. Unusually, on the day he scored his 200th victory he was flying aircraft "Red 23." His victories were marked on "Red 13," however.

A Bf 109 of *Jagdgeschwader* 1 in its blast pen. The pilot is reading while at operational readiness.

In the Defense of the Reich

Bär's next transfer came on 28 December 1943, this time to the *Stabsstaffel* of *Jagdgeschwader 1*, part of the Defense of the Reich based in Rheine. After leading the *6. Staffel* for a time, in February 1944 he was again given command of a *Gruppe*. He took over the *II. Gruppe* of *Jagdgeschwader 1*, succeeding *Hauptmann* Hermann Segatz, who had been killed in action on 8 March 1944. Bär's aircraft was a Fw 190 A-8 with *Werknummer* 431007. It too bore the aircraft number "Red 13." In the period that followed Bär and the *Geschwader* operated from bases in Rheine, Dortmund, Deelen, Stendal, Volkel, Lippstadt, Langenhagen, Echterdingen, Gerlersheim, Fassberg, Oldenburg, Rothenburg, Braunschweig-Waggum, Quedlinburg, Störmede, Gardelegen, Bad Lippspringe Zerbst, Geseke, Detmold, Halberstadt, Paderborn, Erbenheim, and Gütersloh.

After returning to combat, on 28 April 1944 Bär shot down his 200th enemy aircraft, a Liberator. On that day he was flying "Red 23," a Fw 190 A-7 of II./JG 1. "Red 13" continued to wear his victory tally, however.

In March 1944 Bär was made acting *Geschwaderkommodore*, and on 12 May he was named *Kommodore* for a period of eight days, taking the place of the fallen *Oberst* Walter Oesau (1913-1944), the second winner of the Swords. The previous day Oesau, who had 127

On 20 May 1944, *Oberstleutnant* Herbert Ihlefeld (1914-1995, seen here as a *Hauptmann*) was named Bär's successor as *Kommodore* of JG 1. Ihlefeld, an ace of the old guard, veteran of the Spanish Civil War, and wearer of the 9th Oak Leaves with Swords, which he was awarded on 24 April 1942, came from *Jagdgeschwader* 11 and was one of the fighter arm's great leaders.

Unit leaders in the Defense of the Reich during a conference: Bär (2nd from right) with (left) Gustav Rödel (JG 27, 1915-1995) and (right) Kurt Bühligen (JG 2, 1917-1985).

A formation of American B-17 Flying Fortresses over Germany.

victories to his credit, had been shot down and killed over St. Vith in Belgium. In his honor *Jagdgeschwader 1* was given the title "*Jagdgeschwader Oesau*." Knight's Cross wearer *Major* Georg-Peter Eder (1921-1986), a specialist in attacking heavy bombers, took over Bär's *Gruppe* on 13 May 1944.

On 20 May *Oberstleutnant* Herbert Ihlefeld (1914-1995) was named the new commander of the *Geschwader*. An ace of the old guard, Ihlefeld, who had fought in Spain and was the ninth winner of the Oak Leaves and Swords, came from *Jagdgeschwader 11* and was one of the Luftwaffe's great leaders. In more than 1,000 combat missions he had scored 132 victories, including 15 heavy bombers. He would lead the *Geschwader* until the German surrender on 8 May 1945. Heinz Bär's "new" career was not yet over, however.

Defense of the Reich 1944. "Pritzl" Bär, with back to camera, listens as a pilot reports after a mission. On the left is *Hauptmann* Herbert Huppertz (1919-1944) of JG 2, wearer of the 512th Oak Leaves, which was awarded posthumously. Huppertz was killed in France on 8/6/1944 after 70 victories and was promoted to *Major* posthumously.

The Luftwaffe's Last Resurgence

On 1 June 1944, Heinz Bär was named *Kommodore* of *Jagdgeschwader 3* "Udet," succeeding *Major* Karl-Friedrich Müller (*1916), the 126th winner of the Oak Leaves, who had died in a crash on 29 May 1944. Müller, who had only assumed command of the *Geschwader* on 24 March, had 140 victories to his credit, including 51 against western opponents and 17 heavy bombers. He was promoted to *Oberstleutnant* posthumously.

Bär led the *Geschwaderstab* and the *II.* and *III. Gruppen* to France to counter the Allied invasion of Normandy, suffering heavy losses there. In September the units were moved back to the Reich to rest and reequip, but in November the *Geschwader* rejoined the Defense of the Reich, with the *I. Gruppe* flying in the role of high cover and the *IV. Gruppe* serving as a *Sturmgruppe*. From 16 December 1944 the *"Udet" Geschwader* took part in the Ardennes offensive.

On 1 January 1945 Bär was promoted to *Oberstleutnant*, and that same day the Luftwaffe launched "Operation Bodenplatte," its last big operation of the war. At 08:30 Bär took off from Paderborn with the *Geschwaderstab* and the *I. Gruppe*. At the same time 15 aircraft of the *10., 11.,* and *12. Staffel* took off from Bad Lippspringe. Seven more flights from the *IV. Gruppe* took off from Gütersloh. The *Geschwader* formed up over Lippstadt and headed west at low altitude. A Junkers Ju 88 pilot aircraft led the *Geschwader* into Dutch airspace. Its target was Eindhoven and the eleven Allied fighter units stationed there. Although the operation against Eindhoven can be characterized as the most successful of the operation—the 2nd Tactical Air Force lost an entire Canadian Typhoon wing, as well as a considerable number of Spitfires and 25 pilots—*Jagdgeschwader 3* paid a heavy price. All told it lost 18 pilots killed, captured, wounded, or missing, including two *Staffelkapitäne*. This was equal to 22% of the unit's strength, an unacceptable rate of loss for that point in the war. The Luftwaffe's total losses were so great that they could not be made good. "Bodenplatte" cost the lives of two *Geschwaderkommodore*, six *Gruppenkommandeure*, and ten *Staffelkapitäne*. Of the 900 German pilots who took part in the operation, 300 did not come back. On that day *Oberstleutnant* Bär shot down two British aircraft.

On 1 June 1944, Bär was named *Kommodore* of *Jagdgeschwader 3* "Udet," succeeding *Major* Karl-Friedrich Müller, who was killed in a crash.

Major Karl-Friedrich Müller, 126th Oak Leaves (1916-1944), had only been in command of JG 3 since 24 March. Müller, who had 140 victories, including 51 western-flown aircraft and 17 heavy bombers, crashed fatally on 29 May 1944 and was promoted to *Oberstleutnant* posthumously.

Focke-Wulf Fw 190 A-8 of JG 3 prior to the start of "Operation Bodenplatte."

A Consolidated B-24 Liberator takes off on another bombing raid.

B-24 Liberators unload their deadly cargo ...

... and leave the target area. This machine has been hit in one of its engines.

The heavy bomber expert.

Boeing B-17 Flying Fortresses are prepared for another bombing mission over Germany.

A Boeing B-17 Flying Fortress over Berlin during a daylight raid. Tempelhof airport is clearly visible in the upper right corner of the photo.

Above a formation of B-17s, condensation trails left by the escort fighters.

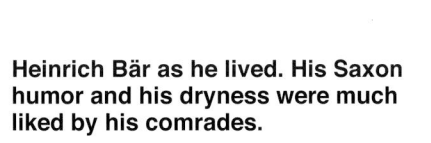

Heinrich Bär as he lived. His Saxon humor and his dryness were much liked by his comrades.

Top Ace in the Me 262

On 14 February 1945, Bär took over *Ergänzungsgruppe 2* based in Lechfeld, near Augsburg. The unit was equipped with the Me 262 jet fighter. His successor as *Kommodore* of *Jagdgeschwader 3* was Oak Leaves wearer *Major* Werner Schroer (1918-1985). Schroer shot down twelve Soviet aircraft in the final weeks of the war and, following his 110th victory, was awarded the 144th Swords on 19 April 1945. *Ergänzungsgruppe 2* had been created from *Erprobungskommando Lechfeld* on 27 October 1944. The instructor pilots of EJG 2 mainly operated against high-flying Allied reconnaissance aircraft, but also tested new versions of the Me 262. Flying a "*Heimatschützer I*," Heinz Bär set an altitude record of 14,700 meters (48,200 ft).

After joining the unit Bär converted to the Me 262. His regular aircraft was a Me 262 A-1a with the aircraft number "Red 13." Under his command the unit retrained Bf 109 and Fw 190 pilots to fly the new type, the world's first operational jet fighter. Bär himself mastered the Me

A formation of B-17 Flying Fortresses carries its deadly cargo to Germany.

Two Me 262 A-1a fighters scramble from Lechfeld.

The "experts" of *Jagdverband* 44. One can identify Johannes Steinhoff (seated) and Walter Krupinski (standing, left).

262 like no other. Even *General* Adolf Galland (1912-1996) was impressed by Bär's ability at the controls of the Me 262. The Allies were not unaware of the activities at Lechfeld, and the airfield was bombed a number of times. As a result, on 23 April 1945 EJG 2 moved to Munich-Riem.

After Bär had flown his first missions from Munich-Riem and scored his first victories flying the Me 262, he asked for a transfer to JV 44, the Me 262 combat unit commanded by the former Inspector and General of Fighters Adolf Galland, who had been relieved by Göring after falling into disgrace. The unit was formed at the end of February 1945, and the Knight's Cross was, so to speak, the "unit emblem" (Galland quotation). A number of successful and well-known fighter pilots joined the unit. Apart from Galland, who wore the Diamonds, JV 44 numbered in its ranks wearers of the highest decorations for bravery, and aces such as *Major* Gerhard Barkhorn (1919-1983, 52nd recipient of the Swords), *Oberst* Günther Lützow (1912-1945, 4th recipient of the Swords), *Hauptmann* Walter Krupinski, *Major* Erich Hohagen, *Major* Wilhelm Herget (1910-1974, 451st Oak Leaves), and *Oberst* Johannes Steinhoff (1913-1994, 82nd recipient of the Swords), just to name a few. The combined victories of the members of JV 44 totaled more than 1,500, and would increase even further by war's end.

"Pritzl" Bär scored his last victory on 26 April 1945, when he took off to intercept an armada of Allied bombers. After *Generalleutnant* Galland was wounded during this mission, along with the death of *Oberst* Günther Lützow two days earlier, on that day *Oberstleutnant* Bär became the last commander of JV 44. The 16 victories he had scored flying the Me 262 made him the most successful jet pilot of the war.

On 8 May 1945 Bär was taken prisoner by the British, but not before he carried out Galland's final order and had all the Me 262s destroyed.

A Me 262 is towed to the runway.

Knight's Cross Profiles   VOLUME 2

A large formation of B-17s over Germany.

Adolf Galland (1912-1996), wearer of the Knight's Cross with Oak Leaves, Swords, and Diamonds. Leader of JV 44, he was demoted from General of Fighters to *Staffel* leader.

Bär beside the tail of "Miss Ouachita."

Major Bär at the crash site of "Miss Ouachita," a B-17 F-70-BO, serial number 23040, which he shot down. With him is his wing man, Leo Schuhmacher.

A contemporary German news caption read: Fighter over the Homeland. Gruppenkommandeur Major Heinz Bär of Leipzig, wearer of the Knight's Cross with Oak Leaves and Swords, is one of our most successful fighter pilots in the west. With a total of 202 aerial victories, 106 Anglo-Americans have fallen to his guns, including 19 Anglo-American heavy bombers.

Messerschmitt Me 262 jet fighters of *Jagdverband* 44 in Munich-Riem.

B-24 Liberator four-engined bomber.

"White 5," a Messerschmitt Me 262 of *Jagdverband* 44.

Heinz Bär on the wing of his Me 262 "Red 13."

An Me 262 of *Jagdverband* 44 is readied for the next sortie.

After a mission against heavy bombers, Bär in front of his "Red 13" of *Jagdverband* 44 in Munich-Riem.

1945: fighter aces with JV 44. From left to right: Erich Hohagen, Bär, and Walter Krupinski.

Left: Bär shortly before he was sent to *Jagdverband* 44.

Heinrich Bär, the most successful jet fighter ace.

The End of the War and the Postwar Period

With just two exceptions, all of the aircraft flown by Heinz Bär bore the aircraft number "13." During the war at least, this number brought him no bad luck; indeed, it was his personal lucky number when one considers that he survived more than 1,000 combat missions and a total of 128 forced landings and bale outs almost unhurt. Between 1939 and 1945 he achieved 221 victories, including 124 against western opponents and 22 heavy bombers. He was the second most successful fighter pilot against the western Allies and holds eighth place on the list of the best fighter pilots.

After he was released from captivity, Bär could not return to his East German home and settled in Brunswick. Waggum airfield in Brunswick, from where he had led *Jagdgeschwader 1* into battle, was to become his second home as an airman.

Bär's popularity, even after the war, was great. After powered flight was again permitted in Germany he served as an aviation advisor. In 1950 he became chairman of the Powered Flight Committee in the German Aero Club e.V. He was also a popular guest and demonstration pilot at air displays. On 5, 6, 7, and 10 May 1956, for example, the county seat of Oldenburg celebrated its annual apple blossom and homecoming festival. The city administration and the cultural-historical society once again tried to offer their guests an interesting and original program. The festival consisted of four days of interesting displays and pleasant coziness. The highlight of Apple Blossom Sunday was a dazzling display of aerobatics over the fair grounds by Heinz Bär. Many of those who were there still remember well the loops, rolls, and inverted maneuvers by the former fighter ace in his Focke-Wulf Stieglitz biplane.

Heinrich Bär at the beginning of the 1950s.

Heinz Bär, the American pilot and author Ray Toliver, and Erich Hartmann (1922-1993, wearer of the 18th Diamonds, 352 victories) in 1956, soon after his release from a Soviet prison camp.

Fatal Crash

Bär also became a test pilot on sporting aircraft that became commercially available after his release. One such machine was the *Zaunkönig* (Wren), an aircraft of light metal construction. The LF 1 *Zaunkönig* was a propeller-driven STOL light aircraft, which had been developed and built under the direction of Professor Hermann Winter at the Brunswick Technical Institute. The aircraft first flew in December 1940, but was destroyed in a crash during flight trials on 11 November 1942. As the military had an interest in a low-speed aircraft for submarine observation and use as an anti-tank weapon and trainer, a second prototype was completed by 1943. After the war the aircraft was taken to Great Britain.

In 1954-55 a third example of the *Zaunkönig* was built in the institute's workshop. Professor Winter hoped that the light-metal aircraft he had designed during the war would now go into production. On 9 June 1955, therefore, he applied to the Federal Aviation Office for type approval. After providing sufficient documentation

The apple blossom festival in Oldenburg in May 1956. The high point of the afternoon on Apple Blossom Sunday was Heinz Bär's breathtaking aerobatics over the fairgrounds. Here is a newspaper clipping.

The Zaunkönig was a popular performer at many air displays in the Federal Republic of Germany in 1955-56. Here it taxis past the terminal building of the Brunswick airport. (HW)

Fighter Pilots with More Than 50 Victories over Western Opponents

Name	Final Rank	Western Victories/Total	Decorations*	Biographical Data	Remarks
Marseille, Hans-Joachim	Hauptmann	158/158	RESB	1919-1942	151 in Africa
Bär, Heinz	Oberstleutnant	125/221	RES	1913-1957	16 on Me 262
Bühligen, Kurt	Oberstleutnant	112/112	RES	1917-1985	40 in Tunisia, 24 heavy bombers
Galland, Adolf	Generalleutnant	103/103	RESB	1912-1996	7 on Me 262
Müncheberg, Joachim	Major	102/135	RES	1918-1943	19 over Malta, 24 in Africa
Schroer, Werner	Major	102/114	RES	1918-1985	61 in Africa
Mayer, Egon	Oberstleutnant	102/102	RE	1917-1944	25 heavy bombers
Priller, Josef	Oberst	101/101	RES	1915-1961	11 heavy bombers
Rödel, Gustav	Oberstlt.	96/98	RE	1915-1995	52 in Africa
Wurmheller, Josef	Major	93/102	RES	1917-1944	18-20 heavy bombers
Schnell, Siegfried	Major	90/93	RE	1916-1944	12 heavy bombers
Rudorffer, Erich	Major	86/224	RES	1917	27 in Tunisia, 12 on Me 262
Oesau, Walter	Oberst	73/127	RES	1913-1944	14 heavy bombers
Reinert, Ernst-Wilhelm	Hauptmann	71/174	RES	1919	51 in Tunisia
Lemke, Siegfried	Hauptmann	69/70	R	1921-1995	21 heavy bombers
Glunz, Adolf	Oberleutnant	69/72	RE	1918-2002	20 heavy bombers
Mölders, Werner	Oberst	68/115	RESB	1913-1941	14 victories in Spain
Eder, Georg-Peter	Major	68/78	RE	1921-1986	36 heavy bombers
Hahn, Hans	Major	66/108	RE	1914-1982	
Hackl, Anton	Major	61/192	RES	1915-1984	34 heavy bombers
Homuth, Gerhard	Major	61/63	R	1914-1943	46 in Africa
Mietusch, Klaus	Major	61/76	RE	1918-1944	16 heavy bombers
Stahlschmidt, Hans-Arnold	Oberleutnant	60/60	RE	1920-1942	all in North Africa
Rollwage, Herbert	Oberleutnant	60/80-85	RE	1916-1980	precise victory total not known
Michalski, Gerhard	Oberstleutnant	59/73	RE	1917-1946	13 heavy bombers
Ihlefeld, Herbert	Oberst	56/132	RES	1914-1995	15 heavy bombers
Seeger, Günther	Major	56/56	R	1918-?	22 in Mediterranean Theater
Wick, Helmut	Major	56/56	RE	1915-1940	
Bendert, Karl-Heinz	Oberleutnant	55/55	R	1914-1983	10 heavy bombers
Galland, Wilhelm-Ferdinand	Major	55/55	R	1914-1943	8 heavy bombers
Schieß, Franz	Hauptmann	53/67	R	1921-1943	21 in North Africa
Hermichen, Rolf-Günther	Major	53/64	RE	1918	26 heavy bombers
Meimberg, Julius	Major	53/53	R	1917	
Kientsch, Willy	Oberleutnant	52/53	RE	1921-1944	16 in Africa, 20 heavy bombers
Pflanz, Rudi	Hauptmann	52/52	R	1914-1942	
Müller, Friedrich-Karl	Oberstleutnant	51/140	RE	1916-1944	17 heavy bombers

*R = Knight's Cross, RE = Knight's Cross with Oak Leaves, RES = RE with Swords, RESB = RES with Diamonds

and blueprints, on 5 October 1955 the Federal Aviation Office issued type approval. It came with a restriction, however: production of the aircraft was not approved. The purpose of the aircraft's flights, even after type approval was issued, was to demonstrate that it was suitable for "self training" by experienced glider pilots. Another objective was approval for the aircraft to be built by flying groups. To this end various changes were proposed which were supposed to be incorporated into the third prototype. This did not happen, however.

On 28 April 1957, exactly 13 years after his 200th victory, retired *Oberstleutnant* Heinz Bär was killed as his family looked on. While Bär was carrying out routine control checks at low altitude over the Brunswick-Waggum airfield, the aircraft went into a spin and crashed from a height of just 50 meters. The eighth-best fighter pilot of all time was one month short of his 44th birthday.

The Zaunkönig (V3). Note the civilian registration D-EBAR.

The end of the third Zaunkönig. On 28 April 1957, the aircraft crashed from a height of 30 to 40 meters during a demonstration of extreme low-speed flight. Its pilot, *Major der Reserve* Heinz Bär, was fatally injured in the crash. (HW)

Sources:
Ralf Schumann Archive, personnel file of H. Bär in the Federal Archives Kornelmünster

Photos:
Ralf Schumann Archive, André Hüsken (Hamburg)

Text and Research:
Ralf Schumann

Acknowledgments:
The author is grateful to Manfred Franzke of UNITEC Media Sales and Distribution, who by publishing this documentation made it available to a wide circle of readers, and to his wife and two sons, who gave up their valuable spare time with their father so that this book could be completed.

Arnold Huebner
The Hero of Bardia

The First *Gefreite* of the
Afrikakorps to Win the Knight's Cross

BY RALF SCHUMANN

Foreword

For Italy, the German Reich's most important ally, the military situation in Libya in the fight against the British Eighth Army had become increasingly desperate. At the urging of the "Duce," Benito Mussolini, on 11 January 1941 Adolf Hitler issued War Directive No. 22 for the formation of a German armored unit and its dispatch to North Africa. Under *General* Erwin Rommel, the Africa Corps saw its first action in March 1941. Later bolstered by units of the Luftwaffe, which provided ground troops and air units, the soldiers of the Africa Corps became symbols of the heroic struggle in the North African theater. One of the many nameless soldiers who did his duty in the blazing heat of the African continent was the Luftwaffe flak *Gefreite* Arnold Huebner.

On 11 March 1942, the press reported on the awarding of the Knight's Cross to two flak soldiers:

Unteroffizier Erich Heintze and *Gefreiter* Arnold Huebner, members of a flak regiment, were put up for the high decoration by the commander-in-chief of Panzer Army Africa, *Generaloberst* Rommel. Through their heroic bravery and determination in the panzer army's battle on the North African front, they demonstrated their prowess in decisive feats of arms, destroying many tanks and taking out enemy battery positions.

Arnold Huebner, the Hero of Bardia who was awarded the Knight's Cross on 7 March 1942, became the first *Gefreite* in the Africa Corps to win this coveted decoration. Huebner, *Gefreite* Emil Berner (1921) – also a flak soldier – and *Soldat* Günther Halm (1922) were the only enlisted men in the North African theater to win the high decoration.

Ralf Schumann

Decorations:

25/05/1941	Iron Cross, Second Class
05/07/1941	Iron Cross, First Class
20/08/1941	Flak Battle Badge
07/03/1942	Knight's Cross of the iron Cross
04/06/1942	German-Italian African Campaign Medal
15/05/1943	"Africa" Cuff Title
27/08/1943	Luftwaffe Ground Battle Badge

Promotions:

Gefreiter
Obergefreiter
Unteroffizier (effective 01/03/1943)
Wachtmeister
Leutnant der Reserve

Participation in Campaigns:

1940/41	Home war zone and Holland
1940	North Africa
1944	Invasion front (France)
1945	Southern Germany (final battles in Reich territory)

6 February 1981: the funeral for Arnold Huebner in the funeral hall of the main cemetery in Gelsenkirchen-Buer. He was buried with military honors, with the Bundeswehr providing the honor guard.

Huebner's coffin, bedecked with the flak of the Federal Republic of Germany, a steel helmet and decorations pillow.

German War Cemeteries in North Africa

Above left: Bordj Cedria, Tunisia (8,652 fallen from the Second World War).
Above right: Deli Abrahim, Algeria (563 fallen of the First and Second World Wars).
Center: El Alamein, Egypt (4,313 fallen of the Second World War).
Bottom left: Tobruk, Libya (6,026 fallen of the Second World War).
Bottom right: Casablanca, Morocco (344 fallen of the First and Second World Wars).

Family and Training

Arnold Huebner was born in Szubn, in the Bromberg District of Posen, on 14 July 1919, the only son of teacher Edmund Huebner, who had won both Iron Crosses as a *Leutnant* and company commander in WWI, and his wife Irene, nee Fulst. After the First World War,[2] in 1919 the area around Bromberg became part of the reformed nation of Poland,[3] and soon after Arnold's birth the Huebner family left their home and settled in Westerholt,[4] in Westphalia. Arnold spent his early childhood there, and in 1924 moved to Gelsenkirchen-Buer, where his father began a new career as a teacher at the Elisabeth School and later the Hindenburg School. From Easter 1924 to Easter 1928 he attended the elementary school in Westerholt, after which he went to the Hindenburg secondary school in Gelsenkirchen-Buer until the end of 1934.

After completing school, on 1 August 1935 Huebner began an apprenticeship[5] as an electician[6] with the Alois Hüttermann Company in Gelsenkirchen-Buer,[7] which he completed on 28 March 1939 before the electrical guild's board of examiners. By then his parents had moved to Krone an der Brahe, where his father was principal of the local girl's school. After successfully taking his journeyman's examination[8] Huebner joined the Reich Labor Service.[9]

Huebner was promoted to *Gefreite* on 1 September 1940.

Labor Service and Call-Up

Huebner did his compulsory tour in the Labor Service from 1 April to 7 September 1939 in Battalion 7/197 in Emlichheim, near Bentheim, and on 8 August 1939 he was transferred to Luftwaffe Construction Company 13/I in Rositten. He subsequently took part in the campaign in Poland with that unit. After being transferred to Luftwaffe Construction Company 45/XII in Kirch-Göns in March 1940 and then to Luftwaffe Construction Company 3/15 XII, on 12 April 1940 he was transferred to the Luftwaffe Flak Artillery and sent to the 1st Battery of Flak Replacement Battalion 11 in Stettin, Pomerania. There he was trained as a gunner.

The flak artillery, which on 1 April 1935 had been moved from the air defense force to the Luftwaffe, became an independent branch of the air force. From then on its branch-of-service color was red.

In 1936, following a visit to the Flak Artillery School in Wustrow, Hitler (1889-1945) decided to greatly expand the flak artillery.

By the end of the war 31 flak divisions and 3 flak searchlight divisions, plus a flak replacement training division and a flak training division had been formed. Thus, by the end of the war there were 158 flak regiments or flak assault regiments and 14 flak brigades, which were combined into seven flak corps. Initially equipped with small 20-mm and 37-mm guns, the flak arm eventually received heavier 88-mm and 105-mm weapons as standard equipment.

As the war went on, the tasks assigned to the flak arm became increasingly varied. In keeping with their general combat role, the deployed batteries were initially employed exclusively in an anti-aircraft role, but later they were used successfully in the direct and indirect fire roles in ground combat. As the war became more difficult, with lasting positional battles and attacks on fortifications, the flak units often became the fire brigades of the army units.

It turned out that the shells of the 88-mm gun could penetrate any tank, and were also effective against enemy bunker positions.

The "Eighty-Eight" became the terror of enemy tanks. More and more frequently the call came from the grenadiers "Flak to the front!" So too in North Africa, where Luftwaffe flak units became increasingly involved in the land battle, supporting their comrades of the army.

4 September 1940: Huebner as a member of Flak Replacement Training Battalion 11 in Stettin, shortly before his transfer to Flak Regiment 33.

Action in the North Africa Theater

Promoted to *Gefreite* on 1 September 1940, on 5 September Huebner was transferred to the I Battalion of Flak Regiment 33, joining the 3rd Battery, and in October of that year he completed a flak gunner course at the Armorer School in Halle.

Initially stationed in Halle-Leuna, Dinslaken, and finally in Holland in 1940 and 1941, the regiment was subsequently ordered to move to Germany. On arriving there, the regiment received further orders to prepare for a move south. The guns were overhauled, new vehicles were sent from all over Germany, and after ten days the regiment moved to its readiness area near Berlin. After another ten days, on 11 February it was ready to march, and the regiment was transferred to the south. Huebner and his unit were being sent to Tripoli[10] (then in Italian, Libya[11]) to join the German Africa Corps.[12]

After a four-day rail journey, Huebner and his comrades arrived in Naples, where the regiment was loaded on ships. From there the steamers put to sea and transported weapons, equipment, ammunition, and men to North Africa. During the crossing the transport Huebner was sailing on was attacked by a British submarine. It fired two torpedoes, but both missed the target.

Three days later, on 20 February 1942, the convoy arrived in Tripoli.

Troop transport en route from Germany to Naples, Italy.

After the ships were unloaded, in the afternoon there was a parade before the commander of the Africa Corps, *Generalleutnant* Rommel. The regiment marched via Homs, Zliten, Nisurata, and Buerat to Sirte. Having reached the Italian front, the regiment went into position.

Huebner began his service in the North African theater with the 3rd Company of Flak Regiment 33. In the weeks and months that followed, he and his battery[13] took part in the fighting in Libya and Egypt.[14]

Since 10 October 1940 the regiment had been commanded by *Hauptmann* Walter Fromm (1910-1999), and under his command Huebner's battalion became one of the most successful flak battalions in the theater. Fromm was awarded the Knight's Cross for this success. He had earlier served as a flak officer in the "Legion Condor" in Spain, winning three Spanish decorations and the German Spanish Cross in Silver with Swords, and was one of the flak arm's most experienced officers.

Historical Background

The German campaign in North Africa was triggered by Italy, which in September 1940 had launched an offensive from its colonial area in Libya against British-held Egypt. Facing defeat, Mussolini sought help from his German ally. Hitler found himself obliged to agree, for a British victory in North Africa, which would enhance its position in the

Members of Flak Regiment 33 during the sea voyage to Tripoli.

Two photos above: arrival in Africa on 20/02/1941.

Outfitting in tropical uniforms.

German warships in the port of Tripoli.

1941. The band of the 115th Infantry Regiment during a public concert for the newly-arrived units of the Africa Corps.

Mediterranean, might result in an invasion of Italy.

On 11 February 1941, German troops under the command of *Generalleutnant* Erwin Rommel landed in Tripoli. These forces, known as the German Africa Corps, began with the recapture of Cyrenaica. Through the successful employment of mobile forces, Rommel was able to drive back the numerically-superior British forces under General Archibald Wavell 800 kilometers. In mid-April 1941, however, lack of supplies halted the German advance at the Egyptian border.

From the first to the last day of the German deployment in North Africa, light and heavy flak units of the Luftwaffe took part in every battle. One of these units was the I Battalion of Flak Regiment 33. It had been the first flak unit sent to Africa. At that time *Gefreite* Arnold Huebner could not know that he would make a name for himself and help establish the battalion's fame in Africa. The first German offensive in Africa began on 31 March 1941.

Hauptmann Fromm reports to Rommel in the port of Tripoli.

Hauptmann Fromm, commander of the I Battalion of Flak Regiment 33, and General Rommel in Tripoli.

Action with the German Africa Corps

Three days later the battalion in which Huebner was serving succeeded in shooting down a British reconnaissance aircraft. After completing a move to the Arco dei Fileni, where the battalion defended the division's assembly area against attacks from land, sea, and air, his battery shot down a Vickers Wellington bomber.

When the German advance in North Africa began in 1941, the 3rd Battery was attached to a reconnaissance battalion and employed against ground targets, with Huebner assigned as gunner on an 88-mm anti-aircraft gun. On that same day the battery shelled British positions near Marsa al Brega with good success, despite enemy counter-fire. The battery subsequently took part in the advance to Agedahia, Solluk, Msus, El Mechili, the encirclement of Tobruk, the occupation of Bardia, the capture of the British airfield at El Adem, and the battles at Capuzzo and Sollum.

At Capuzzo, the Huebner gun was assigned to a motorcycle battalion and, despite heavy fire from enemy naval and land artillery and bombing and strafing attacks, it successfully fought off an attack by eleven enemy tanks and destroyed an enemy battery.

After a series of patrol and assault operations in which Huebner took part

German armored scout cars in Tripoli.

as part of a reconnaissance battalion, on 15 and 16 May his battery successfully repulsed a British attack. For this he was awarded the Iron Cross, Second Class on 25 May 1941.

Huebner took part in the Battle of Sollum from 15 to 18 July, attached to an infantry company. The I Battalion of Flak Regiment 33 distinguished itself in actions during the reconquest of Cyrenaica and the first attack on the Bardia-Sollum front. The 3rd Battery was positioned on Hill 208 between Capuzzo and Sisi Azeiz. The British "Operation Battleaxe" was unsuccessful because the enemy failed to take the decisive Halfaya Pass position and get past Hill 208. On the first day the German position was pounded by British artillery fire. Then three British light tanks attacked. Huebner and his comrades opened fire on them from 1,700 meters and forced the tanks to withdraw. Again the German defensive line was pounded by enemy artillery, and soon afterwards the British readied 25 tanks. When the artillery fire stopped the tanks attacked. The flak gunners allowed the tanks to approach to within 1,000 meters before opening fire. Heavy dust prevented the flak gunners from observing the fall of shot, however. Then the spell was broken; Huebner had knocked out the first enemy tank, which was in flames. He then took aim at the next tank and destroyed it, too. After a half-hour battle the battery had knocked out eight tanks, whereupon

Improvised quarters in Arco dei Fileni, west of El Agheila.

Huebner (left) in a machine-gun post near Arco dei Fileni.

Arco dei Fileni: a letter to the wife at home.

Arco dei Fileni: the "home" of Huebner and his gun crew.

the survivors withdrew to their starting position. Then a German panzer regiment launched a relief attack. After the tanks were withdrawn to another threatened sector the battery found itself facing the next British attack on its own. Once again artillery pounded the position, and fresh enemy tanks joined those already present. A total of 32 enemy tanks faced the battery's position. Then the attack began. This time Huebner's battery waited until the British came within 800 meters. Huebner knocked out a tank with his very first shot, and a wild fire fight began. One tank got to within 70 meters of the German position and opened fire with its machine gun. When Arnold Huebner saw the enemy tank turning its gun on the position he acted instinctively. He input the firing data, quickly aimed his gun, and fired. The tank immediately burst into flames. During the course of the attack he succeeded in destroying seven of the 17 attacking tanks. The British sent more tanks to the point of attack, causing the armada of attackers to grow to 85 vehicles. Ten more drove up five kilometers west of the German strongpoint. The scale of the enemy attack forced the German flak gunners to open fire despite the range. Two tanks were disabled by the battery's concentrated fire, however, the remaining 85 tanks, which had driven up directly in front of the German position, carried on. Then, suddenly, a German panzer regiment struck the enemy from the flank and the attack on the flak battery's position was thwarted.

The next day saw further attacks, all of which were decided in favor of the German defenders. During a counterattack by the 5th Panzer Division on 16 and 17 June towards Capuzzo, Hill 208, and Halfaya Pass, *Hauptmann* Fromm personally directed the 1st and 3rd Batteries, resulting in the destruction of 92 enemy tanks. In a very short time Fromm's battalion had destroyed 169 tanks and 28 aircraft. For this *Hauptmann* Fromm was decorated with the Knight's Cross on 9 July 1941. The commanding general[15] of the Africa Corps, Erwin Rommel[16] (1891-1944), insisted on personally visiting Hill 208 and the brave flak gunners, and gave a brief overview of the situation. For his actions, Arnold Huebner was awarded the Iron Cross, First Class on 5 July 1941. Rommel himself presented the decoration to Huebner on 17 July. On 20 August he was also awarded the Luftwaffe Flak Battle Badge.

Arco dei Fileni, the field kitchen has arrived.

Two photos center: midday meal at Arco dei Fileni.

The reading hour in Arco dei Fileni.

Arco dei Fileni, Huebner repairs his radio set.

The wall relief erected by the Italians at the triumphal arch at Arco dei Fileni over the so-called Via Balbia. It represents the giving of Cyrenaica to King Victor Emanuel II by the Duce.

Spring 1941: the first combat—advance towards El Agheila (three center photos).

Slit trenches near El Agheila.

Erwin Rommel (1891-1944), seen here as a *Generalfeldmarschall*, commander of Panzer Group Africa and later commander-in-chief of Army Group Africa.

An 88-mm anti-aircraft gun after a battle in the North African desert.

An abandoned British armored car in front of Sirte (February 1941).

Huebner (with pith helmet) and comrades while setting up a gun position.

Rest break near Marsa el Brega during the advance.

Center and below: changing a tire on the carriage of an "eighty-eight."

Arnold Huebner was decorated with the Iron Cross, Second Class 25 May 1941.

Hauptmann Fromm and his adjutant, Leutnant Vogel, present Iron Crosses to troops of I Battalion, Flak Regiment 33 following the Battle of Capuzzo and Sidi Azeiz on the Libyan Front.

A heavy prime mover (SdKfz 11), the draught horse of the *Wehrmacht*, with a limbered 88-mm anti-aircraft gun and a load of soldiers in the Libyan desert.

SdKfz 11 of I Battalion, Flak Regiment 33 during the advance in Libya.

An 88-mm anti-aircraft gun with SdKfz 11 prime mover after a battle in Africa.

Shaking the dust out of blankets after a ghibli near Sidi Azeiz, northwest of Capuzzo.

Rommel in the desert.

The German cemetery at the White House in front of Tobruk.

1942: the German Africa Corps on the advance between Tobruk and Sidi Omar.

The battle near Sollum begins.

The desert ablaze!

Hill 208 near Sollum, stocking up on ammunition during the battle.

A photo taken during the tank battle of Sollum.

Patrol operations near Sollum.

Moving out for the counterattack during the Sollum battle.

Near Sollum: rest break during a patrol operation.

Knight's Cross Profiles   VOLUME 2

Sollum, Hill 208: observing the attack.

Sollum, Hill 208: a British Mark IV tank burns.

These two British tanks were also knocked out by Huebner's gun.

Changing positions.

A British Mark IV tank in the field before Hill 208, destroyed by Huebner's gun.

Enemy artillery destroyed in front of Sollum.

A knocked-out German Panzer III tank after the Sollum battle.

Sollum, Hill 208, 88-mm gun in position.

Rest between actions on Hill 208 near Sollum.

A new attack is imminent.

Taking cover in anticipation of another attack.

The battle is over.

Examining a knocked-out British tank.

After the battle there were countless wrecked tanks in front of Hill 208.

Rommel is coming!

Situation report.

Rommel on Hill 208 near Sollum.

The men are enthusiastic.

Examining British equipment after the summer battle for Hill 208 near Sollum.

General Rommel inspects the positions.

For his success in the defense of Hill 208 between Capuzzo and Sidi Azeiz, on 7 July 1941 Huebner was awarded the Iron Cross, First Class on 17 July. He was decorated by Rommel personally.

The successful gunner in front of "his" gun.

After the fighting, a rest break by the sea.

Knight's Cross Profiles — VOLUME 2

Bidding farewell to fallen comrades.

Hauptmann Walter Fromm (1910-1999), commander of I Battalion, Flak Regiment 33, was awarded the Knight's Cross on 9/7/1941 for the success of the units under his command and his personal actions. Fromm was an experienced flak commander who knew how to lead his men in ground actions. He had previously served in the Spanish Civil War and won both Iron Crosses during the Western Campaign in 1940.

Three wearers of the Knight's Cross from Flak Regiment 33. From left: *Oberleutnant* Theodor Schwabach (1912-1981), commander of the 33rd Regiment's 1st Company; *Hauptmann* Walter Fromm; and *Wachtmeister* Reinhard Melzer (1914-1994), a gun commander in the 1st Company. All three won the coveted decoration for their actions in North Africa.

Huebner (center) in North Africa after receiving the Iron Cross, First Class.

VOLUME 2 — Arnold Huebner Profile

An "eighty-eight" of the I Battalion of Flak Regiment 33 in action against land targets.

Before it goes on, a letter to the wife.

On 20 August 1941, Huebner was awarded the Luftwaffe Flak Battle Badge.

The battalion commander briefs his men before the next action.

123

The Knight's Cross

On 18 November 1941, the 3rd Battery was attached to the 21st Panzer Division in Bardia. Through his personal bravery and determination, Huebner knocked out another fifteen British tanks and one artillery battery. In the Battle of Sidi Azeis Huebner destroyed eight tanks in twenty minutes. One tank was just 70 meters away when it was knocked out. By then the gunner was personally responsible for the destruction of 24 tanks and an artillery battery. *Generaloberst* Erwin Rommel, commander-in-chief of Panzer Army Africa, subsequently put *Gefreite* Huebner and *Unteroffizier* Erich Heintze (1916-1998), a gun commander in the same battery, up for the Knight's Cross. Huebner and his comrades subsequently took part in more and fiercer battles. I Battalion of Flak Regiment 33 was almost wiped out in the fighting of November 1941 and had to be withdrawn from action, and then from the North Africa theater. In February 1942 the remnants of 3rd Battery, Flak Regiment 33 were withdrawn to Germany to rest and reequip.

Huebner, one of few members of the regiment not killed or captured, was given home leave, which he spent with his parents in Bromberg, to where they had returned after the German occupation of Poland. Then, on 7 March 1942, as a result of a recommendation by Rommel, Arnold Huebner was awarded the Knight's Cross[17] of the Iron Cross for his actions in the fighting of November 1941. Gun commander *Unteroffizier* Erich Heintze was also awarded the prestigious decoration that same day.

The press release cited in the foreword was issued on 11 March 1942.

A newspaper article about Arnold Huebner published after the Battle of Sollum.

November 1941. Huebner (foreground) during a pause in the action on the North African front.

A SdKfz 7 of I Battalion, Flak Regiment 33 following a strafing attack by British aircraft.

September 1941: "The African."

September 1941: Huebner with "eighty-eight" and crew.

January 1942: time to rest and recover after the battalion was pulled out of the front line.

The Ju 52 was also invaluable in North Africa, flying supplies in to the Africa Corps and flying out wounded soldiers or men going home on leave.

February 1942. Flight to Germany to collect replacements and equipment from Leipzig. The men, including Huebner, would be back in North Africa by the summer of 1942.

February 1942: Huebner during a stop in Sicily during the flight to Germany.

Back in Germany

On 15 March 1942, in Leipzig, *Generalleutnant* Walter Feyerabend (1891-1962), commander of the 14th Flak Division, presented the Knight's Cross to Arnold Huebner and *Unteroffizier* Erich Heintze. Not yet 23 years old, Huebner was the first *Gefreite* of the Africa Corps to receive the decoration.

On 1 June 1942 Huebner was promoted to *Obergefreite*, and on 4 June he was awarded the Memorial Medal of the German-Italian Campaign in Africa. His return to the African theater was brief, for from 16 July to 5 September 1942 he attended a non-commissioned officer course and was subsequently ordered to join an anti-tank course at the flak artillery school in Stolpmünde. He thus avoided the total destruction of his 3rd Battery during the following retreat. The 1st and 2nd Batteries went down fighting at Halfaya Pass. Because of his combat experience, however, Huebner was soon released from the course.

On 21 October 1942 he was transferred to the 1st Battery of Motorized Flak Regiment 33 (tropical), in which he served as a gunner until 3 November. After a transfer to Flak Replacement Battalion 9 (tropical) in Fürth and a several-month stay in hospital to recover from a tropical illness, on 26 March 1943 he was promoted to *Unteroffizier*, and on 15 May 1943 was awarded the "Africa" cuff band.

Arnold Huebner married Ingeburg Hinzmann on 27 July 1943. The marriage would produce four children: a son and three daughters.

On 27 August 1943 he was awarded the Luftwaffe Ground Battle Badge, a visible recognition of the actions in which he had taken part.

With the 1st Battery of Flak Training Battalion 697 (tropical) in Fürth, Huebner was transferred to the invasion front in the Tours[18] area of France.[19]

Huebner, who had been promoted to *Wachtmeister* on 1 April 1944, returned to combat following the Allied invasion of Normandy[20] on 6 June 1944. Huebner and his gun were attached to various units and took part in fighting against Allied troops. Near Versoul, in France, Huebner destroyed his 25th enemy tank, an American Sherman. In the summer Huebner was withdrawn from the front. In October 1944 he completed an armorer course in Halle and took officer candidate training at the officer school in Kitzingen, and from January 1945 took part in the land battle on German territory with Flak Replacement Battalion 39 in Coblenz.

In February 1945 Huebner was transferred to Nuremberg[21] with a battery from the flak battalion just before the Americans entered the city. There the officer candidate organized an all-round defense[22] of the city by the flak[23] on behalf of its military commander.[24] After the Americans encircled Nuremberg, Huebner led a breakout from the beleaguered city by 40 members of his battery. Near Ingolstadt[25] he joined up with a 105-mm flak battery and, acting as an artillery observer, he directed its fire during the defense of the Danube crossing[26] in that area. The subsequent retreat by German forces took Huebner through Freising[27] and Erding[28] and further to the south.

On 7 March 1942, Arnold Huebner was awarded the Knight's Cross of the Iron Cross for his heroic actions in Africa. It was Rommel who recommended him for the decoration.

Leipzig, 15 March 1942: ceremonial presentation of the Knight's Cross to Huebner and *Unteroffizier* Heintze by General Feyerabend, commander of the 14th Flak Division. Here the general welcomes the assembled troops.

15 March 1942: presentation of the Knight's Cross to *Unteroffizier* Erich Heintze.

Presentation of the Knight's Cross to Arnold Huebner. General Feyerabend places the prestigious decoration around Huebner's neck.

The general congratulates the two recipients after presenting them their interim award certificates.

Reviewing the troops.

General Feyerabend congratulates soldiers of Flak Regiment 33 for their heroic actions in the North African theater.

The battalion commander congratulates Huebner on receiving the Knight's Cross.

Arnold Huebner was awarded the Knight's Cross of the Iron Cross on 7 March 1942, becoming the first *Gefreite* in the Africa Corps to receive the decoration.

Unteroffizier Erich Heintze (1916-1998) was also awarded the Knight's Cross on 7 March 1943. Heintze was a gun commander in Flak Regiment 33's 3rd Battery, and like Huebner played a decisive role in the battery's and the battalion's success.

EIN GESCHICHTLICHES VOLK VEREHRT IN SEINEN SOLDATEN DIE TUGENDEN DES MUTES DER EHRE UND DER TREUE

Hauptmann IHLEFELD

Der Führer verlieh dem Hauptmann Herbert Ihlefeld, Gruppenkommandeur in einem Jagdgeschwader, anläßlich seines 101. Luftsieges, als neuntem Offizier der deutschen Wehrmacht, das EICHENLAUB MIT SCHWERTERN ZUM RITTERKREUZ DES EISERNEN KREUZES

General d. Fl. BOGATSCH — **General d. Fl. FÖRSTER**

Oberleutnant SPÄTE

Der Führer verlieh dem Oberleutnant Wolfgang Späte, Staffelkapitän in einem Jagdgeschwader, als 90. Soldaten der deutschen Wehrmacht, das EICHENLAUB ZUM RITTERKREUZ DES EISERNEN KREUZES

WIE SIE DAS RITTERKREUZ ERWARBEN

General der Flieger Bogatsch, General der Luftwaffe beim Oberkommando des Heeres, ist es u. a. zu danken, daß die dem Oberbefehlshaber des Heeres unterstehenden Flieger- und Flakartillerieverbände jederzeit den Anforderungen gerecht wurden, die an sie auch im Erdkampf gestellt werden. — General der Flieger Förster, Kommandierender General eines Fliegerkorps, hat sich durch zielbewußten und wohldurchdachten Kräfteeinsatz in der Führung des ihm unterstellten Fliegerkorps und während der Kämpfe in der Sowjetunion hervorragende Verdienste erworben. — Oberst im Genst. Koller, Chef des Generalstabes einer Luftflotte, schuf durch seine wohlüberlegten Vorschläge und Anordnungen, die sich durch Kühnheit des Wagens auszeichneten, die Voraussetzungen für die Erfolge der Luftflotte im Feldzug gegen Frankreich und im Kampf gegen England. — Major Kuno Hoffmann, Kommandeur in einem Kampfgeschwader, versenkte mit seiner Gruppe im Südosteinsatz Mai 1941 insgesamt 257 000 BRT und beschädigte 276 000 BRT schwer, darunter einen Kreuzer und einen Zerstörer. — Hauptmann Krebs, Batteriechef in einem Flakregiment, zeigte an der Ostfront in zahlreichen schweren Kämpfen höchste Einsatzbereitschaft. Von einer schweren Verwundung noch nicht genesen, eilte er zu seiner Batterie zurück, an deren Spitze er erneut hervorragende Waffentaten bei der Abwehr feindlicher Angriffe vollbrachte. — Hauptmann Wittmer, Gruppenkommandeur in einem Kampfgeschwader, erwarb sich im Kampf gegen England besondere Verdienste durch die Bekämpfung feindlicher Flugplätze und die Zerschlagung von Anlagen der Luftrüstungsindustrie. Die von ihm und seiner Besatzung auch im Osten durchgeführten Tiefangriffe haben sich vielfach entscheidend für die Operationen der Erdtruppen ausgewirkt. — Hauptmann Petersen, Staffelkapitän in einem Kampfgeschwader, führte in den Abwehrkämpfen auf der Krim zahlreiche Tiefangriffe auf feindliche Kolonnen und Nachschubstraßen durch und fügte dem Gegner so schwere Verluste zu, daß die eigene Abwehrfront entscheidend entlastet wurde. — Hauptmann Ihrig, Staffelkapitän in einem Kampfgeschwader, gelang es u. a., in zweimaligem Nachtangriff ein bedeutsames Rüstungswerk bei London zu zerstören. Auf dem Flugplatz Pinsk hat er in sechs Tiefangriffen 60 Feindflugzeuge vernichtet. — Oberleutnant Klien, Flugzeugführer in einem Kampfgeschwader, vernichtete an der Ostfront u. a. in schneidigen Tiefangriffen zahlreiche Feindflugzeuge am Boden, Transportzüge und Eisenbahnanlagen. — Oberleutnant Schwegler, Staffelkapitän in einem Kampfgeschwader, gelang es u. a., vor Kreta einen Zerstörer schwer zu beschädigen und im Schwarzen Meer einen Sowjetkreuzer durch Volltreffer zu zerstören. Außerdem hat er insgesamt 116 000 BRT versenkt bzw. schwer beschädigt. — Oberleutnant Schweickardt, Staffelkapitän in einem Sturzkampfgeschwader, hat im Ostfeldzug durch Vernichtung von Flugzeugen, Panzern, Marschkolonnen und Transportzügen den Sowjets großen Schaden zugefügt. — Oberleutnant Sattler, Flugzeugführer in einem Sturzkampfgeschwader, gelang es, auf der Halbinsel Krim starke feindliche Truppenansammlungen zu zersprengen und einen Panzerzug, 11 Flak- und Artilleriestellungen sowie 50 Fahrzeuge zu vernichten. — Oberleutnant Fritz Schulze, Staffelkapitän in einem Zerstörergeschwader, hat als Schlachtflieger auf dem nordafrikanischen Kriegsschauplatz unermüdliche Einsatzbereitschaft und kühnes Draufgängertum bewiesen. — Leutnant Bliesener, Flugzeugführer in einem Kampfgeschwader, ist der Typ eines kühnen Draufgängers. Zweimal hinter den sowjetischen Linien abgeschossen, hat er sich mit seiner ganzen Besatzung zu den eigenen Linien wieder durchgeschlagen, um mit ungebrochener Willenskraft sofort wieder ins Flugzeug zu steigen. — Leutnant Omert, Flugzeugführer in einem Jagdgeschwader, erzielte bisher 40 Luftsiege und zerstörte 18 Feindflugzeuge am Boden. — Leutnant Dickfeld, Flugzeugführer in einem Jagdgeschwader, schoß in harten Luftkämpfen 47 Feindflugzeuge ab, zerstörte 8 sowjetische Flugzeuge am Boden, 11 Lokomotiven und 2 Panzer. — Feldwebel Roßmann, Flugzeugführer in einem Jagdgeschwader, hat bisher in mehr als 250 Feindeinsätzen 42 feindliche Flugzeuge abgeschossen. — Gefreiter Huebner, Richtkanonier in einer Flakbatterie, schoß in Nordafrika in wenigen Minuten acht Panzer ab. Insgesamt hat er als Richtkanonier 21 Panzer vernichtet.

Oberst KOLLER — Major HOFFMANN
Hauptmann KREBS — Hauptmann WITTMER
Hauptmann PETERSEN — Hauptmann IHRIG
Oberleutnant KLIEN — Oberleutnant SCHWEGLER
Oberleutn. SCHWEICKARDT — Oberleutnant SATTLER
Oberleutnant SCHULZE — Leutnant BLIESENER
Leutnant OMERT — Leutnant DICKFELD
Feldwebel ROSSMANN — Gefreiter HUEBNER

The Luftwaffe magazine "Der Adler" (The Eagle) reported on the awarding of the Knight's Cross to Arnold Huebner in a special edition issued in June 1942.

With members of 3./FlaKRgt 33 in Leipzig.

Knight's Cross wearer Huebner describes his experiences in Africa at a meeting of the NSLB District Administration Bromberg.

Huebner and his bride Ingeburg with representatives of the city of Westerholt. Second from the right is Mayor Hambach.

Addressing students at his former school in Westerhold, Huebner describes his actions in Africa that won him the Knight's Cross.

Knight's Cross Profiles   VOLUME 2

Wenn wir am Lautsprecher sitzen

und Frontberichte hören, können wir uns die „andere Seite", die für den Bericht sorgt, nicht so recht vorstellen. — Hier sehen wir, wie es gemacht wird: Ein Rundfunk-Kriegsberichter unterhält sich mit den Ritterkreuzträgern Unteroffizier Heintze und Gefreiten Hübner und läßt sich über ihre Erlebnisse berichten.

(PK-Aufn.: Kriegsberichter Eisenhart)

Several of the contemporary newspaper articles that reported on the awarding of the Knight's Cross to Arnold Huebner.

Zwei von der Flak (deren große Erfolge im gegenwärtigen Kriege ein besonderes Ruhmesblatt bilden): Ritterkreuzträger Unteroffizier Heintze und Ritterkreuzträger Gefreiter Hübner.
PK-Aufn.: Kriegsberichter Eisenhard (PBZ.)

On 1 June 1942 Huebner was promoted to *Obergefreite*.

Arnold Huebner and his fiancé Ingeburg Hinzmann, whom he married on 24 July 1943.

June 1942. Back in Africa, but only for a short time.

Huebner attended a non-commissioned officer course at the Flak Artillery School in Stolpmünde from 16 July to 5 September 1942. The photo shows him with some classmates.

For his actions in the North African theater, Huebner was awarded the newly-created Italo-German Campaign Medal in Africa on 4 June 1942.

Non-commissioned officer candidate course in Stolpmünde. Here Huebner is in conversation with the course director.

Huebner during the non-commissioned officer's candidate course in Stolpmünde.

Generalfeldmarschall Albert Kesselring. His *Luftflotte* 2 provided the Africa Corps with air support.

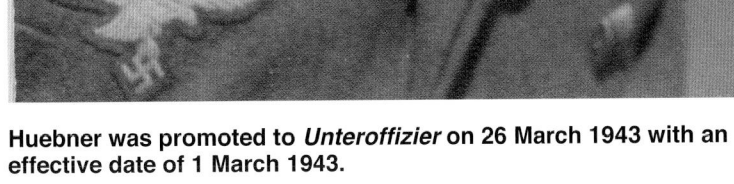

Huebner was promoted to *Unteroffizier* on 26 March 1943 with an effective date of 1 March 1943.

On 15 May 1943 Huebner was awarded the "Africa" cuff title.

Huebner was awarded the Ground Combat Badge of the Air Force on 27 August 1943.

October 1943: Huebner as a member of the 1st Battery of Flak Training Battalion 697 (tropical) in Fürth.

As an *Unteroffizier* and gunner on an 88-mm anti-aircraft gun.

Autumn 1943: *Unteroffizier* Huebner with an *Unteroffizier* of the flak artillery and wearer of the German Cross in Gold.

On 4 May 1944, Oblt.d.R. Ewald Quest, commander of the 1st Battery of Flak Regiment 33 (mot.), became the last member of the regiment to win the Knight's Cross. He was awarded the decoration while serving on the Eastern Front.

Major **Walter Fromm**, geboren am 2. Februar 1910 vernichtete mit seiner Abteilung in kurzer Zeit 169 Panzerkampfwagen und 29 Flugzeuge.

Ihm wurde am 9. Juli 1941 das Ritterkreuz des Eisernen Kreuzes verliehen wegen eines schlachtentscheidenden Einsatzes seiner Einheit im Verlauf der Sollumschlacht vom 15. – 17. Juni 1941.

Unteroffizier **Erich Heinze**, geboren am 27. September 1916 vernichtete mit seinem Geschütz als Geschützführer zusammen 30 Panzerkampfwagen und eine Art.-Batterie, davon 7 Panzer im Feldzug gegen Frankreich und 23 Panzer während der Kämpfe in der Sollumschlacht 41 und der Winterabwehrschlacht 1941/42 in Nordafrika.

Ihm wurde am 7. März 1942 das Ritterkreuz des Eisernen Kreuzes verliehen.

Obgefr. **Arnold Huebner**, geboren am 14. Juli 1919 vernichtete als Richtkanonier an einem 8,8 cm-Geschütz 24 Panzerkampfwagen und 1 Artilleriebatterie in den harten Kämpfen Nordafrikas bei der Sollumschlacht 1941 und der Winterabwehrschlacht 1941/42 in Nordafrika.

Ihm wurde für hervorragende Leistungen am 7. März 1942 das Ritterkreuz des Eisernen Kreuzes verliehen.

This flyer bearing the images of Fromm, Heintze,. and Huebner was handed out on Armed Forces Day 1943 (two-page folding sheet).

The troops also trained with captured vehicles. Here Huebner is climbing out of a French-made truck.

In October 1944, Huebner completed an armorer course in Halle and was then ordered to the officer candidate school in Kitzingen for officer training.

On 1 March 1944 Huebner was promoted to the rank of *Wachtmeister*.

Winter 1944: *Wachtmeister* Huebner (3rd from right) with members of his class during the officer training course at the officer candidate school in Kitzingen.

Beginning of 1945: Huebner as a member of Flak Replacement Battalion 39 at the Deutsches Eck and in front of Fortress Ehrenbreitstein in Coblenz.

Knight's Cross Profiles　　VOLUME 2

What might he have been thinking?

1945: an "eighty-eight" in the ground role.

Action in southern Germany.

Examining a captured American truck.

Captivity and the Postwar Period

On 5 May 1945 Arnold Huebner, who had been promoted to *Leutnant* on 1 May but did not learn of it until after the war, was captured by the Americans in Waging am See, in Upper Bavaria. He was not a POW for long, however, being released on 24 June 1945.

Like many of his comrades, Huebner now had to fashion a civilian existence in the postwar period, which as a wearer of the Knight's Cross was not easy at first. Arnold Huebner settled in West Germany,[29] and on 19 January 1949 took his examination for a master's certificate as an electrician at the chamber of commerce in Münster. On 1 January 1950 he started an electrical installation company in Gelsenkirchen-Buer. On 31 December 1972 the operation was turned into a limited company and operated successfully internationally. Huebner thus displayed energy and drive in civilian life. Arnold Huebner, who always stayed in touch with his former comrades and was a welcome guest at reunions, died on 1 February 1981 in Gelsenkirchen. Since then his son Manfred has run the company. Arnold Huebner's funeral was held in the funeral hall of the main cemetery in Gelsenkirchen-Buer. He was buried with military honors, with an honor guard from the *Bundeswehr* present. There was a large attendance as the first *Gefreite* of the Africa Corps to be decorated with the Knight's Cross of the Iron Cross was carried to the grave. (see page 101.)

An early gathering of the Order of Knight's Cross Wearers (O.d.R.) in the 1960s. Huebner (center) with fellow wearers of the Knight's Cross, including General der Panzertruppe (Rtd.), Walter K. Nehring (front row, 4th from left), and *Generalleutnant* (Rtd.) Horst Niemack (front row, 2nd from left).

Order of Knight's Cross Wearers gathering in the 1970s. Huebner (left) and members of the order. Among those in the photo is General (Rtd.) Horst Niemack, a holder of the Swords, Knight's Cross holder Alois Schnaubelt, Oak Leaves wearer Martin Steglich, and Knight's Cross holder Max Haschberger.

1977: Huebner with members of the O.d.R. celebrating the birthday of a comrade.

The Knight's Cross Wearers of Flak Regiment 33

(in order of when the decoration was awarded)

Name/Final Rank	Theater of War	On	Biographical Data
Melzer, Reinhard Wachtmeister	Uffz., gun commander in 1.*/FlaKRgt 33 in Africa	30/06/1941	1914-1994
Schwabach, Theo Hauptmann	Oblt., commander of 1./FlaKRgt 33 in Africa	30/06/1941	1912-1981
Fromm, Walter Major	Hptm., commander of I.**/FlaKRgt 33 (mot.) in Africa	09/07/1941	1910-1999
Heintze, Erich Oberwachtmeister	Uffz., gun commander in 3./FlaKRgt 33 (mot.) in Africa	07/03/1942	1916-1998
Huebner, Arnold Leutnant der Reserve	Gefr., gunner in 3./FlaKRgt 33 (mot.) in Africa	07/03/1942	1919-1981
Quest, Ewald Hauptmann der Reserve	Oblt.d.R.***, commander of 1./FlaKRgt 33 (mot.) on the Eastern Front	04/05/1944	1915-1971

* Battery   ** Battalion   *** the Reserve

1979: Arnold Huebner during celebrations marking his sixtieth birthday.

1979: Huebner on his sixtieth birthday, surrounded by members of the O.d.R.—North Rhine-Westphalia Group. Present were Knight's Cross wearers Alexander Uhlig, Martin Steglich, Hans Fiedler, Alois Schnaubelt, Heinz Lotze, Karl-Heinz Molinari, and the birthday boy.

Arnold Huebner (X) with his employees.

Arnold Huebner died on 1 February 1981 following a brief illness.

> Aus seinem schaffensfrohen, von Liebe und Sorge für seine Familie erfüllten Leben, ist heute mein lieber Mann, unser guter Vater, Schwiegervater, Großvater, Bruder, Schwager und Onkel
>
> ## Arnold Huebner
> Elektromeister
> Ritterkreuzträger
>
> * 14. 7. 1919   † 1. 2. 1981
>
> für immer von uns gegangen.
>
> Freundschaft und Hilfsbereitschaft waren ihm ein Herzensbedürfnis.
>
> In stiller Trauer:
>
> **Ingeburg Huebner** geb. Hintzmann
> **Klaus Presse**
> **und Frau Gudrun** geb. Huebner
> **Fritz Mühlnickel**
> **und Frau Ingrid** geb. Huebner
> **Manfred Huebner**
> **und Frau Ria** geb. Hesterkamp
> **Anke Huebner**
> **Enkel Oliver, Gerrit, Jeanine, Anika, Vanessa und Verena**
>
> 4660 Gelsenkirchen-Buer, Hülser Straße 9
>
> Die Trauerfeier findet statt am Freitag, dem 6. Februar 1981, um 9 Uhr in der Trauerhalle des Hauptfriedhofes. Daran anschließend ist die Beisetzung.
>
> Von Beileidsbezeigungen am Grabe bitten wir Abstand zu nehmen.
>
> Allen, denen aus Versehen keine besondere Nachricht zuging, diene diese als solche.

Sources:

Ralf Schumann Archive, contemporary reports
Private property and estate of Leutnant (Rtd.) Arnold Huebner (+)

Text and Research:

Ralf Schumann

Photos:

Ralf Schumann Archive, estate of Leutnant (Rtd.) Arnold Huebner (+

Acknowledgments:

The author is especially grateful to Ingeburg Huebner, who made this publication possible by providing access to her late husband's papers, documents and photos. I am also grateful to Manfred Franzke of UNITEC Media Sales and Distribution, who by publishing this documentation made it available to a wide circle of readers, and to his wife and two sons, who gave up their valuable spare time with their father so that this book could be completed.

Hyperlinks:

1 "http://de.wikipedia.org/w/index.php?title=G%C3%BCnther_Halm&action=edit" \o "Günther Halm"
2 "http://de.wikipedia.org/wiki/Erster_Weltkrieg" \o "Erster Weltkrieg"
3 "http://de.wikipedia.org/wiki/Polen" \o "Polen"
4 "http://de.wikipedia.org/wiki/Westerholt" \o "Westerholt"
5 "http://de.wikipedia.org/wiki/Lehre" \o "Lehre"
6 "http://de.wikipedia.org/wiki/Elektriker" \o "Elektriker"
7 "http://de.wikipedia.org/wiki/Gelsenkirchen-Buer" \o "Gelsenkirchen-Buer"
8 "http://de.wikipedia.org/wiki/Gesellenpr%C3%BCfung" \o "Gesellenprüfung"
9 "http://de.wikipedia.org/wiki/Reichsarbeitsdienst" \o "Reichsarbeitsdienst"
10 "http://de.wikipedia.org/wiki/Deutsches_Afrikakorps" \o "Deutsches Afrikakorps"
11 "http://de.wikipedia.org/wiki/Tripolis" \o "Tripolis"
12 "http://de.wikipedia.org/wiki/Libyen" \o "Libyen"
13 "http://de.wikipedia.org/wiki/Batterie_%28Milit%C3%A4r%29" \o "Batterie (Militär)"
14 "http://de.wikipedia.org/wiki/%C3%84gypten" \o "Ägypten"
15 "http://de.wikipedia.org/wiki/Kommandierender_General" \o "Kommandierender General"
16 "http://de.wikipedia.org/wiki/Erwin_Rommel" \o "Erwin Rommel"
17 "http://de.wikipedia.org/wiki/Ritterkreuz" \o "Ritterkreuz"
18 "http://de.wikipedia.org/wiki/Tours" \o "Tours"
19 "http://de.wikipedia.org/wiki/Frankreich" \o "Frankreich"
20 "http://de.wikipedia.org/wiki/Normandie" \o "Normandie"
21 "http://de.wikipedia.org/wiki/N%C3%BCrnberg" \o "Nürnberg"
22 "http://de.wikipedia.org/wiki/Stadtkommandant" \o "Stadtkommandant"
23 "http://de.wikipedia.org/wiki/Rundumverteidigung" \o "Rundumverteidigung"
24 "http://de.wikipedia.org/wiki/FlaK" \o "FlaK"
25 "http://de.wikipedia.org/wiki/Ingolstadt" \o "Ingolstadt"
26 "http://de.wikipedia.org/wiki/Donau" \o "Donau"
27 "http://de.wikipedia.org/wiki/Freising" \o "Freising"
28 "http://de.wikipedia.org/wiki/Erding" \o "Erding"
29 "http://de.wikipedia.org/wiki/Deutschland" \o "Deutschland"

Joachim Müncheberg

The Hunter of Malta

BY RALF SCHUMANN AND
WOLFGANG WESTERWELLE

Foreword

With 135 victories, Major Joachim Müncheberg was one of the most successful fighter pilots of WWII. Despite this success – almost all of which he achieved against the Western Allies – his name has always been somewhat overshadowed by other aces like Adolf Galland, Werner Mölders, and Hans-Joachim Marseille.

This great fighter pilot is best characterized by the following quote (from T*he Famous Me 109*):

… Müncheberg as a superior.
His ability to always recognize immediately the heart of a problem was more impressive than his individual feats in combat. His men followed the youthful and intelligent unit leader without hesitation. While he was extremely disciplined and conscious of duty himself, he always had understanding for the weaknesses and mistakes of others, for he demanded from no one what he could not do himself…

Ralf Schumann

Decorations:

00/11/1939	Iron Cross, Second Class
00/05/1940	Iron Cross, First Class
00/00/1940	Wound Badge in Black
14/09/1940	Knight's Cross of the Iron Cross
07/05/1941	Italian Gold Medal of Bravery "Medagalia d'Oro"*
07/05/1941	Knight's Cross of the Iron Cross with Oak Leaves (12th)
17/03/1942	Operational Flying Clasp for Fighter Pilots in Gold
15/06/1942	German Cross in Gold
09/09/1942	Knight's Cross with Oak Leaves and Swords (19th)

*First foreign recipient

Promotions:

01/08/1937	Unteroffizier
16/12/1937	Fähnrich
13/09/1938	Oberfähnrich
08/11/1938	Leutnant
19/07/1940	Oberleutnant
19/09/1941	Hauptmann
30/11/1942	Major

Combat Missions:

500 combat missions over the Western Front, England, the Channel Front, the Mediterranean, Malta, Sicily, the Balkans, Libya, the Eastern Front, North Africa, Tunisia.

Victories:

135 victories, of which 33 were scored in the east (with Stab/JG 51), 19 over Malta, 1 in Yugoslavia and 24 in North Africa, including 46 Spitfires.

Positions Held:

23/09/1938 – 31/08/1939	pilot in I./Jagdgeschwader 234
01/09/1939 – 22/09/1939	pilot in 10.(Nachtjagd)/Jagdgeschwader 26
23/09/1939 – 22/08/1940	adjutant in headquarters of III./Jagdgeschwader 26
22/08/1940 – 17/09/1941	Staffelkapitän 7./Jagdgeschwader 26
19/09/1941 – 21/07/1942	Kommandeur II./Jagdgeschwader 26
22/07/1942 – 27/09/1942	Kommodore Jagdgeschwader 51 (acting)
01/10/1942 – 23/03/1943	Kommodore Jagdgeschwader 77

Types Flown Operationally:

Messerschmitt Bf 109 E-7
Messerschmitt Bf 109 G-2
Messerschmitt Bf 109 G-6
Focke-Wulf Fw 190 A-1
Focke-Wulf Fw 190 A-2

Graphic: Manfred Franzke

Bf 109 E-7 "White 12." *Oberleutnant* Joachim Müncheberg, *Staffelkapitän* 7./JG 26, February 1941.

Bf 109 E-7 "White 1." *Oberleutnant* Joachim Müncheberg, *Staffelkapitän* 7./JG 26, March 1941.

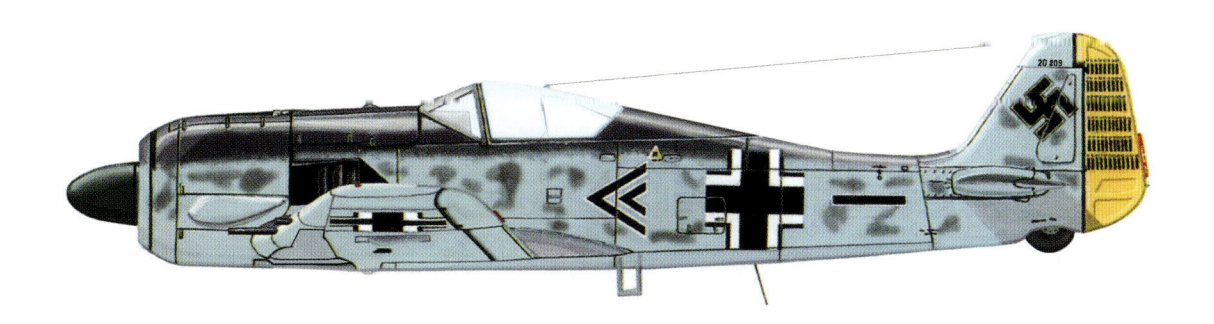

Focke-Wulf Fw 190 A-1. *Hauptmann* Joachim Müncheberg, *Kommandeur* II./JG 26, December 1941, Werk-Nr. 20209.

Childhood and the Desire to Fly

Joachim Müncheberg came from Pomerania. He was born in Friedrichshof, Dramburg District, on 31 December 1918, the only son of landowner and *Rittmeister* (Retired) Paul Müncheberg. In contrast to many of his classmates, he found school very easy and to him it was fun. He soon discovered his love of sports. Whenever possible he took part in sporting activities. He was both an enthusiastic decathlete and a passionate handball player. His interests went even deeper, however.

Another passion soon awakened in "Jochen": flying! His cousin Hermann Hackbusch was partly responsible for this, for the former World War flyer (Baltic States) often took him flying from Staaken airport in Berlin. It became obvious that the boy would catch the love of flying.

As fate would have it, Hermann Hackbusch was killed on one of his flights on 14 October 1933 at the age of just 38 years, but that in no way dampened "Jochen" Müncheberg's enthusiasm for flying. He had just one goal; to sit at the controls himself.

But first there was school. From 1928 to 1936 he attended the secondary school in Dramburg. Following graduation he completed two months in the Labor Service.

"Jochen" Müncheberg grew up in the Dramburg District of Pomerania and spent his childhood and school years there. Aerial photo of Dramburg.

From 1928 to 1936 he attended the secondary school in Dramburg. Here a view of the marketplace, with St. Marien Church.

Another scene from Dramburg. On the left is St. Marien Church and the war memorial.

Start of His Air Force Career

Müncheberg subsequently began his air force career. It was clear that he would follow the career path of an officer like his father (by then a *Major* of the Reserve). He began his service on 4 December 1936, joining the Luftwaffe officer training school in Dresden as a *Fahnenjunker* (officer candidate). Basic military training was followed by a variety of courses which slowly brought Müncheberg closer to his dream of being in the cockpit, even if at first it was the dual controls of an ungainly biplane trainer at which the ambitious officer candidate had to prove himself. But even the longest training had its conclusion. On 1 August 1938 he was promoted to *Unteroffizier*.

Following promotion to *Oberfähnrich* on 13 September 1938, on the 23rd Joachim Müncheberg went to Cologne to join the *I. Gruppe* of the then *Jagdgeschwader 234*, which on 1 November 1938 became an independent command and was renamed JG 132. Soon afterward the *Geschwader* was awarded the title "*Schlageter.*" On 1 May 1939 the unit received its ultimate title of *Jagdgeschwader 26 "Schlageter."*

At 01:00 on 25 August 1939, as part of German mobilization, the two *Jagdgruppen* were ordered to Bönninghardt (Wesel area, Moers) and Odendorf (Eifel). The headquarters of JG 26 also moved to Odendorf. It initially set up its command post in Palmersheim Castle.

Müncheberg began his military service as a *Fahnenjunker* (officer candidate) at the Luftwaffe officer school in Dresden.

On the day the war broke out (1 September 1939), there was another reorganization of the *Geschwader*. A new Staffel, *10. (Nachtjagd) Jagdgeschwader 26*, was formed under the command of *Oberleutnant* Johannes Steinhoff (1913-1994). Müncheberg, who had been promoted to *Leutnant* on 8 November 1938, was assigned to the new unit. His attachment to the *Staffel* was brief, however, for on 23 September he was transferred to the newly-formed *III. Gruppe* (*Hauptmann* Walter Kienitz until 31/10/1939, then *Major* Baron Ernst von Berg) as adjutant.

The *Geschwader*'s *III. Gruppe* was formed in Werl under *Hauptmann* Walter Kienitz. It consisted of elements of the headquarters companies of the first two *Gruppen*, the *2.* and *4. Staffel* of *Jagdgeschwader 26*, the *4.*, *5.*, and *6. Staffel* of *Zerstörergeschwader 26*, and the airfield operating companies of ZG 26.

When it was formed, the *Gruppe* had only sufficient aircraft for a single *Staffel* and most were older types: eight Arado Ar 68s, four Bf 109s, two Klemm 35s, and one Arado Ar 66. In October 1939, the Arado Ar 68s and the older Bf 109s were turned in and replaced with 30 modern Messerschmitt Bf 109 Es.

Thus, during the early phase of the war *Jagdgeschwader 26* consisted of the *Geschwaderstab* with headquarters company and three *Gruppen*. Each *Gruppe* consisted of a headquarters with a staff flight and three *Staffeln* each with twelve aircraft.

Luftwaffe Officer School Dresden, part of the former auditorium building.

After completing his training he received the pilot's badge.

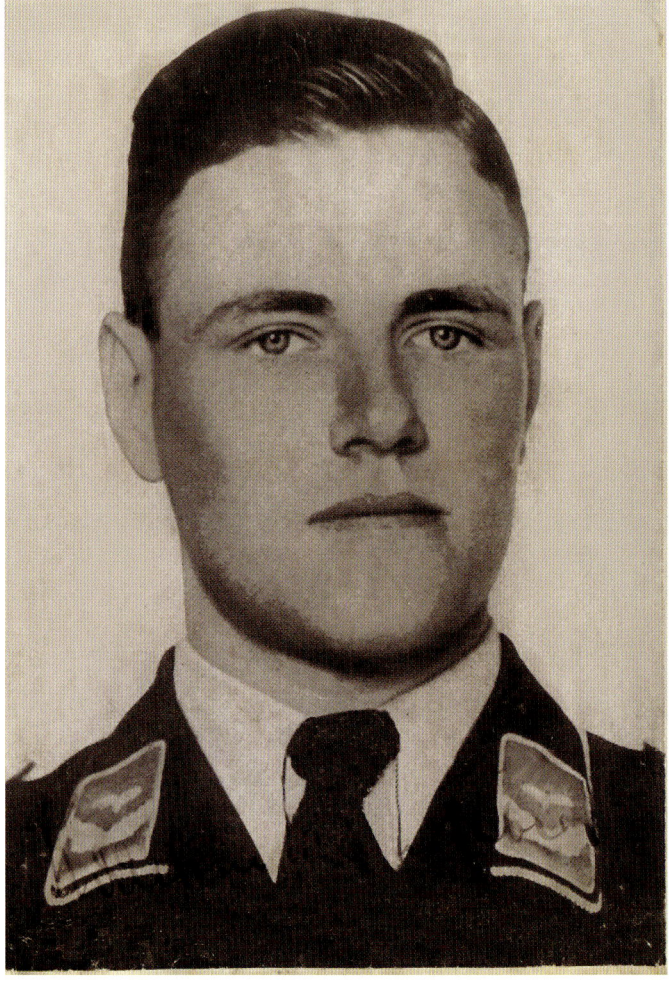

The young *Leutnant* Müncheberg, promoted on 8 November 1938.

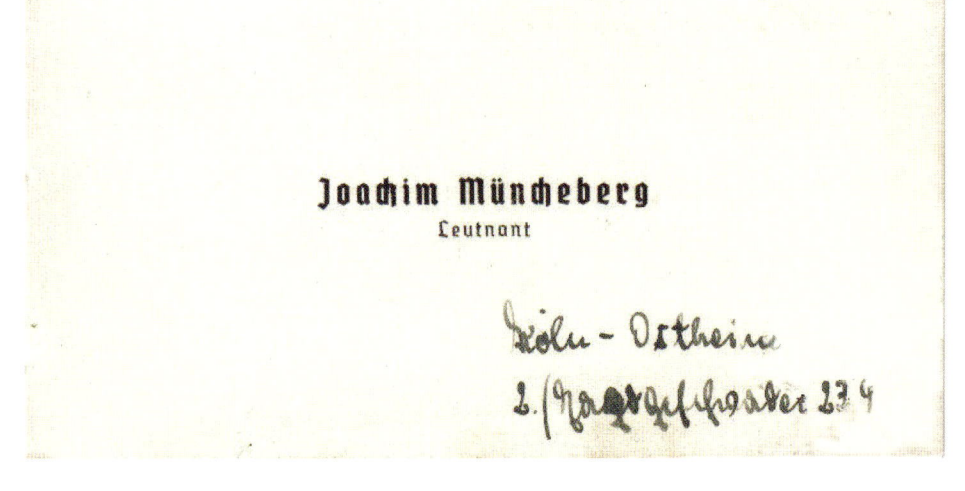

One of *Leutnant* Müncheberg's business cards from his time in Cologne-Ostheim with 2./JG 234.

Sitzkrieg in the West

While the bulk of the Luftwaffe played an active role in the blitzkrieg against Poland, *Jagdgeschwader 26*'s mission was "Defend the Ruhr region with its vital industries and guard the western frontier."

Translated, this meant endless hours of cockpit readiness and patrols along Germany's western frontiers. Crossing the border was strictly forbidden, and Belgian-Dutch neutrality was to be respected.

There was excitement on 2 September when several aircraft appeared over Bönninghardt, and two days later when a British aircraft that had come in over neutral Holland dropped leaflets. It was later found out that these "propaganda flights" were in reality a cover for aerial reconnaissance.

Otherwise it was very quiet in the west between autumn 1939 and spring 1940. There were only isolated incursions, usually by single aircraft. It is not surprising, therefore, that the entire *Geschwader* was only able to shoot down two enemy aircraft by 9 May 1940. One of the victories was scored by *Leutnant* Bürschgens of *I.*

Blenheim bombers. Müncheberg shot down an aircraft of this type for his first victory on 7 November 1939.

Gruppe on 28 September in a dramatic combat with eleven Curtiss P-36s which ignored the reconnaissance aircraft he was escorting.

The *Geschwader*'s second went to Joachim Müncheberg of *III. Gruppe*, who achieved his first success in aerial combat on 7 November. His victim was a Bristol Blenheim I of 57 Squadron RAF, which went down southwest of Opladen. The crew baled out, and Müncheberg was awarded the Iron Cross, Second Class for his success.

For his first victory he was awarded the Iron Cross, Second Class in November 1939.

Müncheberg's second victory was over a Curtiss Hawk H 75 A like the one seen here.

Blitzkrieg in the West and First Successes

In the early morning hours of 9 April 1940, the German *Wehrmacht* launched a combined-arms attack against Denmark and Norway ("Operation Weserübung"), and soon afterwards the "Sitzkrieg" in the west also came to an end.

The campaign in the west against the Netherlands, Belgium and Luxembourg (Case Yellow), and France (Case Red) began on 10 May 1940. The rapid advance by German ground forces received decisive support from the Luftwaffe, including the *III. Gruppe* of *Jagdgeschwader 26*. Joachim Müncheberg recorded his second victory at 17:45 on 11 May northwest of Antwerp. His victim was a Curtiss Hawk 75A, an American design in service with the *Armée de l'Air*. It was the only French opponent Müncheberg would claim during the campaign against France. After that all of his victims were British, either Hurricanes or Spitfires. As well, on the afternoon of 31 May 1940 he shot down a Westland Lysander tactical reconnaissance aircraft in the Dunkirk area. On 6 June 1940 Adolf Galland (1912-1996, the second man to be decorated with the Knight's Cross with Oak Leaves, Swords, and Diamonds on 28/1/1942) was named *Kommandeur* of *III. Gruppe* of *Jagdgeschwader 26 "Schlageter."* By the time the guns fell silent on 25 June 1940, Müncheberg had shot down eight enemy aircraft and wore the Iron Cross, First Class (awarded him in May) on his flight jacket.

Spring 1940, Bf 109 Es of JG 26.

Müncheberg scored his 6th victory on 31 May 1940, when he shot down a Westland Lysander.

In May 1940 he received the Iron Cross, First Class.

Fighting over the Channel and Rise to Fighter Ace

After the rapid victory over France and the British Expeditionary Corps' hasty flight from Dunkirk, the German side was both surprised and at a loss as to what to do. There were no plans at all for a landing in England, nor did the military have the necessary equipment. As a land power, Germany had never concerned itself with large-scale amphibious warfare, a role for which the *Kriegsmarine*, hopelessly inferior to the Royal Navy, was ill-suited.

Nevertheless, Germany was now compelled to act, and plans for a major landing on the British Isles, dubbed "Operation Sea Lion," were hastily devised. The army and navy had very different ideas about how this should happen, but from the outset one thing was clear: the Luftwaffe would have to clear the way for an invasion and achieve air superiority, at least over the English Channel. To achieve this goal, it was first necessary to weaken the Royal Air Force and its ground organization as much as

Generalfeldmarschall Milch (in leather coat) visits the *Geschwader* in France. Behind Milch is "Jochen" Müncheberg.

Müncheberg was awarded the Wound Badge in Black in 1940.

Mission briefing with the commander of *III. Gruppe*, *Oberleutnant* Schöpfel, and the *Staffelkapitän* of 7./JG 26, *Oberleutnant* Müncheberg, at the end of August in Caffiers, France.

The new *Kommandeur* in conversation with officers of the *Gruppe*. 2nd from right is "Jochen" Müncheberg.

The *Geschwader* has turned out for an inspection by the Commander-in-Chief of the Luftwaffe. On the left is *Kommodore* Galland. On the right wing, the *Kommandeur* of II./JG 26 "Jochen" Müncheberg.

6 September 1940, Caffiers, France. 17 victory bars adorn the tail of Müncheberg's Bf 109 E.

possible. Attacks would also be made against industrial targets, ports, and shipping.

The Luftwaffe command immediately developed and implemented the necessary orders, and in July the buildup of bomber and fighter units for an aerial offensive against England began.

From mid-July to the end of the month *Jagdgeschwader 26* moved its three *Gruppen* to the following airfields:

I./JG 26:	Audembert
II./JG 26:	Marquise-East
III./JG 26:	Caffiers

Then, on 30 July the *Geschwader* headquarters also moved to Audembert, while its command post went to Le Colombier. The unit's aircraft were fitted with armor plates to protect the pilot's head and recognition markings were painted on the wing tips. The latter were changed each evening.

Soon afterwards the pitiless duel between the Luftwaffe and the Royal Air Force began. For the English it was a struggle for survival, for the Germans a fight against time. If "Operation Sea Lion" was to happen at all, the landings would have to be carried out before the autumn storms. There was not much time for the planned defeat of the British air force.

In the first phase, which began in July, the Luftwaffe stepped up operations

1940: Bf 109 Es of 8./JG 26 in Caffiers, France.

Joachim Müncheberg Profile

Müncheberg was promoted to *Oberleutnant* on 19 July 1940.

On 14 September 1940, Müncheberg was awarded the Knight's Cross of the Iron Cross after twenty victories.

Müncheberg as *Staffelkapitän* of 7./JG 26, a position he had held since 22 August 1940.

Schöpfel, Galland, and Müncheberg, the first three Knight's Cross wearers of JG 26.

Müncheberg claimed a Bloch 151 for his 21st victory on 17 October 1940.

against coastal convoys and shipping in the Channel. This was essentially a job for the dive-bomber units, which required fighter escort to be effective. Soon the pilots of *Jagdgeschwader 26*, who all too frequently had to carry out escort missions, were simply called "Channel flyers." The British side also had a nickname ready, "Channel Boys." Later they became the "St. Omer Boys" and then "Abbéville Boys."

On 19 July 1940, Müncheberg received preferential promotion to *Oberleutnant* for exceptional achievements.

Müncheberg's first victim during the aerial campaign against England was a Hurricane, which he shot down 15 kilometers northeast of Dover on 28 July 1940. It was victory number ten for the newly-promoted *Oberleutnant*.

The Battle of Britain

While *I.* and *II. Gruppe* were flying "*freie Jagd*" (offensive fighter sweeps) in the Maidstone area, during which *Leutnant* Borris scored two victories, on "*Adlertag*" (Eagle Day) *III. Gruppe* operated over the Channel as far as Dover, its primary task being to provide air cover for air-sea rescue aircraft and motor torpedo boats – a relatively quiet affair.

One day later, however, it became fully involved. The *Gruppe* was ordered to take part in a raid against the port of Dover, flying escort for three *Stuka-Gruppen.*

Escorting the slow dive-bombers was an unpopular task among the aggressive fighter pilots, but it did result in contact with the enemy.

III. Gruppe claimed six victories on 14 August 1940, shared between *Major* Galland, *Oberleutnant* Müncheberg, *Oberleutnant* Beyer, *Oberleutnant* Schöpfel, *Leutnant* Bürschgens, and *Leutnant* Müller-Dühe.

Müncheberg's victim was a Hurricane (either of 32 or 615 Squadron), which went down near Folkestone at 13:29.

15 August saw the *Gruppe* provide escort for bombers of *Kampfgeschwader 1 "Hindenburg"* and *2 "Holzhammer."* Widespread fighting developed, in the course of which Müncheberg was able to shoot down a Spitfire of 64 Squadron shortly after 16:00.

Channel Coast of France. The new Knight's Cross wearer and *Oberleutnant* with his comrades.

Galland, Schöpfel, Müncheberg (3rd from left, seated), and other officers of JG 26 while studying maps.

Christmas 1940: Adolf Hitler visits JG 26 on the Channel Coast. In the photo from the left: Oblt. Spick, Hptm. Adolph, Hptm. Pingel, Hitler, *Oberstleutnant* Galland, Hptm. Schöpfel and, in the foreground with his back to the viewer, Oblt. Müncheberg.

On 22 August, the 28-year-old *Major* Adolf Galland assumed command of the *Geschwader* and Müncheberg was named *Kapitän* of *7. Staffel* of *Jagdgeschwader 26*.

On 24 August 1940, a Sunday, the *Geschwader* escorted bombers attacking targets south of London. At 12:22 Müncheberg shot down a Hurricane of 151 Squadron over Ashford.

On 31 August, another Hurricane fell to Müncheberg's guns at precisely 10:00 northwest of Braintree. It was his 15th victory, and number 16 followed the next day at 14:52 west of Goodhurst. Once again it was a Hurricane.

Joachim Müncheberg shot down his twentieth enemy aircraft late on the afternoon of 14 September south of Maidstone. His success was mentioned in the *Wehrmacht* communiqué of 15 September. The day before Müncheberg had been awarded the Knight's Cross of the Iron Cross on the occasion of his twentieth victory. He became the third member of the *Geschwader* to receive the coveted decoration after Adolf Galland and Gerhard Schöpfel (1912-2003), the *Staffelkapitän* of 9./JG 26.

The Situation in the Mediterranean Theater in Early 1941

At the beginning of 1941, the Mediterranean region increasingly came into the focus of future combat operations, even though that theater had not figured in Germany's original war plans.

While Adolf Hitler was fixated on the Soviet Union and his coming war of aggression there, Italian dictator Benito Mussolini had developed his own big power plans.

On 28 October 1940, the "Duce" presented the Greek Prime Minister Joannis Metaxas with an unacceptable ultimatum, and several hours later sent his troops into Greece. Hitler had previously tried in vain to talk the fascist leader out of the attack, and now found himself forced to act by the actions of his ally, for the Italian offensive drew in the British, who immediately sent troops and air force units to Greece. These forces were not all that strong, but their psychological impact was not lost on friend or foe. As well, the Italian offensive was a total failure and became bogged down at the very outset.

The developing situation forced Germany to intervene, for the new British air bases represented a danger to the buildup against Soviet Russia and posed a threat to the Rumanian oil fields so vital to Germany's war machine.

On Friday, 13 December 1940, Hitler signed Directive No. 20, the operations plan for "Operation Marita," the attack on Greece.

The German plans were not implemented, however, for further developments in the military situation, triggered by her ally Italy, made German intervention in the region unavoidable, especially because the "Duce" had launched further military adventures, all of which turned into disasters. In August 1940 he initiated an attack against British Somaliland which turned into a debacle, as did the attempt to invade Egypt from Libya in September 1940.

The "Duce" had no better luck in the war at sea. While he had always claimed the Mediterranean to be *"mare nostrum"* (our sea), he also suffered a bitter reversal there.

On the night of 11-12 November 1940, British torpedo-bombers from the aircraft carrier *Illustrious* attacked the Italian battle fleet at anchor off Taranto. Three priceless battleships were badly damaged. The *Conte di Cavour* was never put back in service, while the *Littorio* and *Caio Duilio* were put out of action for six months. As a result, the British were able to run their convoys through the Mediterranean to Malta and Crete without the threat of attack by Italian surface units. This increasingly shifted the balance of forces away from parity—to the disadvantage of the Axis powers. The German side reacted reluctantly, forming a "blocking unit" to restore the situation on the African front. Erwin Rommel, a panzer general who had won fame during the war against France, was placed in command of

Müncheberg shot down his first bomber, a Vickers Wellington, on 15 March 1941. It was also his 32nd victory.

Treviso Sant' Angelo. Müncheberg's Messerschmitt Bf 109 E-7 during a fuel stop by 7./JG 26 during its move to Sicily. There are 23 victory bars on the aircraft's rudder.

Oberleutnant **Müncheberg's Bf 109 E in Treviso Sant' Angelo.**

anti-shipping units, however, the number of bomber aircraft was inadequate for the task, at least at first. As well, the corps had to cover a very large area, and the wide variety of missions led to a dispersal of its forces. In addition, in the beginning the only fighter unit available to *General* Geißler was *Hauptmann* Kaschka's *III./Zerstörergeschwader 26*, which was equipped with the twin-engined Messerschmitt Bf 110 C. Out of necessity this *Zerstörergruppe* became a "maid of all work," and was used to provide fighter escort for the bombers and air cover for convoys. This aircraft type was ill-suited for at least the latter task. No single-engine fighter aircraft were available in this area of operations, however, all that changed at the beginning of February 1941.

the *Deutsche Afrikakorps* (German Africa Corps). Shipped from Italian ports, the first units arrived in Libya in February 1941.

From the beginning, the German command was conscious of the threat to supply transports crossing the Mediterranean posed by the powerful British fleet and the Royal Air Force. On the island of Malta it had an unsinkable aircraft carrier "in the flesh of the Axis." Malta had been developed into a major fleet and air base that threatened German-Italian supply convoy traffic to North Africa. The British fighters stationed on the island were obsolete, but not to be underestimated. Aircraft hangars built into the rock were invulnerable to air attack.

To safeguard the supply transports, Malta had to be eliminated as a base of operations. An airborne invasion of the island was considered, but was infeasible in the short term. It was therefore decided to "neutralize" Malta through massive air attacks.

On 10 December 1940, the *Wehrmacht* High Command (OKW) issued a directive for the *X. Fliegerkorps* under *General der Flieger* Geißler to move to Sicily and Sardinia. The Stuka and bomber formations attached to the air corps were specialized

March 1941: Müncheberg's Bf 109 E-7 "White 12" with 30 victory bars on its rudder (Gela, Sicily).

Sicily, spring 1941. One of 7./JG 26's Bf 109 Es is readied for a sortie.

Operations in the Mediterranean Theater

On 9 February 1941 the *Staffel*, led by *Oberleutnant* Müncheberg, arrived in Gela, Sicily. Equipped with new Bf 109 E-7 fighters, the *Staffel's* pilots were all veterans who had earned their spurs in the air battles of the western campaign and the Battle of Britain. Müncheberg then flew aircraft "White 12" with the *III. Gruppe* bar. The *Staffel* emblem consisted of a red heart painted on both sides of the engine cowling.

Just three days after arriving on the "lemon island," Müncheberg achieved his first success in the Mediterranean theater. Over Malta on the afternoon of 12 February he shot down a Hurricane of 261 Squadron. Four days later another Hurricane from the same squadron became Müncheberg's milestone victory: number 25! Just seven minutes later, at 10:45, he shot down another Hurricane, again from 261 Squadron, east of Ta Venezia. And so it went on. The airspace over and around Malta became a productive hunting ground for the ambitious fighter pilots. By the end of March Müncheberg added six more Hurricanes and a Wellington to his victory total.

The March 28, 1941, was a special day for Joachim Müncheberg, for on that day he recorded his 33rd victory during his 200th combat mission. His victim was another Hurricane of 261 Squadron, which went down 10 kilometers south of Gozo at 17:30. It was reason for the entire *Staffel* to celebrate. Soon afterwards the *Staffel* had to pack up again, but this time the move would be a short one.

The German campaign against Yugoslavia and Greece began on 6 April 1941, and the Luftwaffe was assigned to provide air support for the army units.

That day Müncheberg and his *Staffel* moved to Tarent, and from there flew missions over the Balkans. On 8 April the unit moved back to Gela with one more victory on Müncheberg's account. On the first day of operations (6 April) he claimed a Fury biplane of the JKRV shot down northeast of Podgorica at 12:05, and another Fury and a Breguet XIX destroyed on the ground. In reality, the Furys were Avia BH-33s. Only the Yugoslavian aircraft shot down in air combat was confirmed.

The flying visit to the Balkans was brief, and Müncheberg's unit soon returned to operations against Malta; for Rommel's *Afrika-Korps* had begun its attack toward Tobruk and was dependent on the supply convoys which repeatedly came under attack from Malta.

The sky over the picturesque Mediterranean island became Müncheberg's favorite hunting ground. Late on the afternoon of 11 April 1941 he destroyed two more Hurricanes of 261 Squadron in a matter of minutes. He recorded another victory on the evening of 23 April. Soon afterwards there was another somewhat different action.

Sitting beside his Bf 109 E-7, one of 7./JG 26's pilots observes returning German aircraft at Gela airfield in Sicily.

A Bf 109 of 7./JG 26 taxies past an Italian CR 42 which is having its machine-guns bore-sighted.

28 March 1941, Gela airfield, Sicily. Müncheberg returns from his 200th combat mission, during which he scored his 33rd victory.

Leutnant Mietusch congratulates Müncheberg on his success.

Oberleutnant Müncheberg describes his most recent combat.

The event was celebrated accordingly.

The latest success has been added to his victory tally on his aircraft's rudder.

Joachim Müncheberg

Müncheberg in the cockpit prior to taking off on another mission over Malta. Assisting in takeoff preparations is his maintenance crew chief.

A scene from the Battle of Malta. Pilots of 7./JG 26 study a map taken from a downed British pilot. Seated, partially concealed, and wearing a forage cap is *Staffelkapitän* Müncheberg.

On 27 April a Bf 109 F-5 reconnaissance aircraft spotted a Short Sunderland four-engined flying boat at anchor in Kalafrana Bay (Malta). With too few bombers available and immediate action required, Müncheberg's fighters were alerted. Soon afterwards seven Bf 109 E-4s disappeared into the sky in the direction of Malta. A low-level approach was chosen so as to avoid detection by British radar. Just short of the target Müncheberg began to climb. The remaining Messerschmitts followed like a string of pearls before diving one after another on the huge target. Despite heavy fire from light anti-aircraft guns, the flying boat was easy prey. When the last Messerschmitt disappeared over the horizon, all that was left in the harbor on Kalafrana Bay was a heap of burning wreckage. Acknowledged as a victory, the destruction of the flying boat was credited to the entire *7. Staffel* instead of to a single pilot.

May 1, 1941, was another particularly successful day for Joachim Müncheberg. Three more enemy aircraft went down before his guns. Despite hazy weather the German fighters were in the air early—and the opposition on the island wasn't sleeping either. It was still breakfast time (07:53) when Müncheberg shot down a Hurricane southeast of St. Paul's Bay. Two minutes later a second Hurricane went down in flames southwest of Ta Venezia. It was his 40th victory.

Müncheberg's Bf 109 E-7 of 7./JG 26 on Pantelleria airfield.

Müncheberg and Carola Höhn, actress and wife of Knight's Cross wearer Arved Crüger (1911-1942).

161

Müncheberg's "White 12" is rearmed …

… and fitted with a long-range tank. The tip of the propeller spinner is painted white, the *Staffel* color. The engine cowling is painted pale yellow back to the engine firewall. A red heart adorns both sides of the engine cowling.

Here is Müncheberg's own description of this air combat:

I was flying with my *Kette* along the north coast of the island of Malta. Despite the haze, I suddenly spotted a squadron of Hurricanes right in front of us. I immediately hauled my crate around and flew roughly in the direction of the sun. The Hurricane squadron split up into two groups, each of four machines. The first four came on an opposite course, while the second group flew towards Malta. The Tommies apparently hadn't seen us. I calmly positioned myself behind the second group. The British "tail-end Charlie" zigzagged wildly, but apparently either failed to see us or mistook us for friendly aircraft.

A brief transmission to my number three in the *Kette*: "Keep an eye on the enemy lookout." Then I moved in to attack the closest of the enemy flight. The range was slightly too great when I opened fire. Emitting a thin smoke trail, he rolled to the right and dove away, disappearing into the mist. My attack on the second was better. He had obviously also failed to notice us, for he calmly flew straight as a board in front of me. My bursts of fire chewed up his fuselage, and he went down burning fiercely. Beside me I saw my wingman (Lt. Johannsen) pursue the third Hurricane until big pieces also flew from its fuselage. The mortally wounded Tommy went down trailing a long banner of smoke. To my right, the obviously excited lookout turned towards my wing man. I hauled my crate around and fired a short burst across the enemy's nose, and when the fellow put his nose down and dove away I made a head-on firing pass from above. After we both pulled up we again approached each other head-on, and several seconds later the Tommy was above to my right and tried to attack me from above and behind. I immediately dove away to the south, and as I did so I saw another Hurricane at about 100 meters, apparently intent on landing. I immediately made the decision to go after him.

My attack came completely by surprise, and the first burst must have hit the pilot, because the machine flew along in front of me, weaving gently and taking no evasive action, obviously no longer under control.

Pilots of 7./JG 26 in Sicily. Left Müncheberg, in the center *Leutnant* Klaus Mietusch (1918-1944).

I fired my last shells at the enemy from a distance of 50 meters. Its left wing burning fiercely, the Tommy dropped away below me.

It was now high time to get away, for I was all alone, and not only did I see the "tail-end Charlie" from before, but the black and white bellies of four more Hurricanes as well. At the same time the anti-aircraft guns had woken up and had begun firing wildly. I breathed a sigh of relief when I had escaped from that witch's cauldron. My concern for my two comrades proved unwarranted. Together we are now celebrating this lovely success.

Late that afternoon, at 17:15, Joachim Müncheberg shot another Hurricane out of the sky—his 41st victory.

The *Wehrmacht* communiqué of 1 May 1941 declared:

Last night German bombers and dive-bombers again attacked the port of La Valetta on Malta and the Venezia airfield with good success. Three Hurricane fighters were shot down in air combat over the island on the morning of 1 May … In fighting over the island *Oberleutnant* Müncheberg achieved his 39th and 40th victories. (Note: The victory in the late afternoon came too late for this OKW report.)

On 6 May 1941 Müncheberg shot down two more enemy aircraft, once again Hurricanes of 261 Squadron.

The Messerschmitt with the yellow nose, the red heart, and the number 12 was now equally famous and feared. By now it was also known on both sides of the front, not least because of broadcasts by the military radio station in Catania.

On 7 May Joachim Müncheberg became the 12th recipient of the Knight's Cross with Oak Leaves. His actions in the Battle of Malta also resulted in him becoming the first foreigner to be awarded the Italian Gold Medal of Bravery. The only other foreign recipient of the highest Italian decoration was Hans-Joachim Marseille (1919-1942), a fighter pilot who gained fame as the "Star of Africa" and became the fourth recipient of the Knight's Cross with Oak Leaves and Diamonds.

7./JG 26 in Sicily. In the foreground on the far right is *Leutnant* Mietusch. The unit's Bf 109 E-7s are serviced and ready for action.

On 7 May 1941, Müncheberg became the twelfth recipient of the Knight's Cross with Oak Leaves.

Müncheberg after returning from the awarding of the Oak Leaves.

On 7 May 1941, Müncheberg became the first German soldier to receive the Italian Gold Medal of Bravery "Medagalia d'Oro," seen here beneath the Operational Flying Clasp.

This retouched collector's postcard was issued by Rhön after Müncheberg was awarded the Oak Leaves …

… as was this Hoffmann photo collector's card.

Müncheberg claimed his 68th and 69th victories in an air battle over the Channel. Here the great fighter pilot demonstrates that he is also master of the horn.

Hauptmann Müncheberg returned to the Channel Coast wearing the Oak Leaves and assumed command of III. Gruppe of JG 26. Kommodore Galland used the occasion to invite him on a pheasant hunt. The party includes Oberst Huth (1896-1962), Galland, Müncheberg, and Erbo Count von Kageneck (1918-1942), Staffelkapitän of 9./JG 27. On 26/10/1941 von Kageneck became the 39th recipient of the Oak Leaves.

Joachim Müncheberg Profile

Proud wearer of the Oak Leaves.

In full war paint.

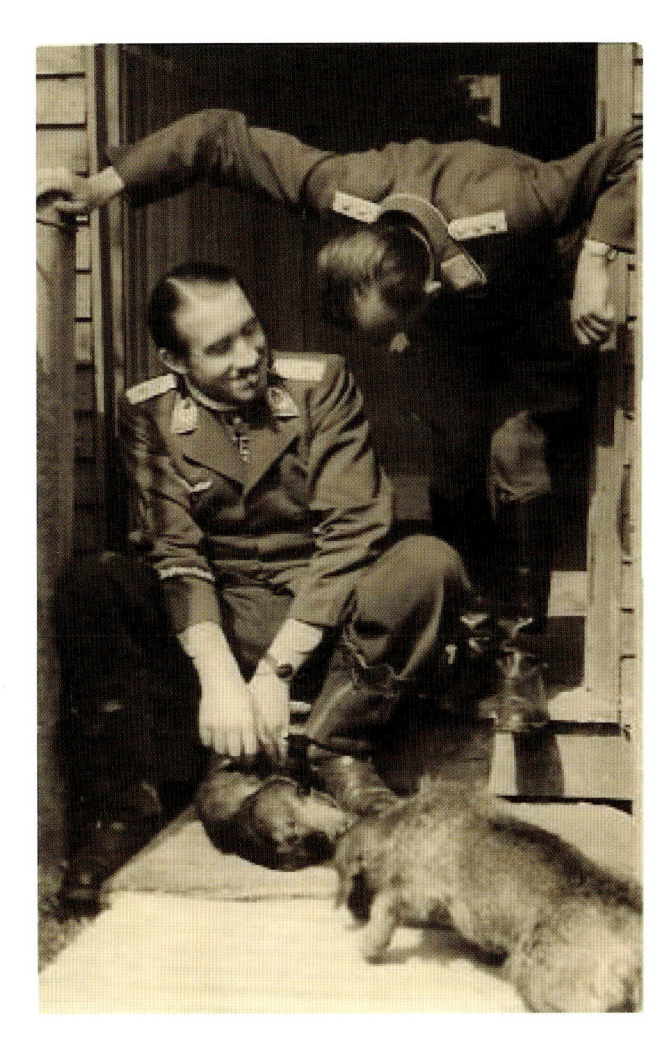

Even the "old man" enjoyed playing with the dogs.

Joachim Müncheberg with a member of the *Gruppe* and the two dogs Seppl and Pitt.

First Air Battles in North Africa

On 1 June 1941, six aircraft of *7. Staffel* (without tropical equipment) made the jump from Sicily to the "dark continent." The purpose of the move was to temporarily bolster the Axis air forces in preparation for the attack on Tobruk and subsequent advance in the direction of Egypt.

The new base of operations for Müncheberg and his men was the forward airfield at Ain el Gazala, located on Bomba Bay between Derna and Tobruk.

7./JG 26 was temporarily attached to I./JG 27, whose commander was the extremely popular *Hauptmann* Eduard Neumann (1911-2004). The welcome for the newcomers was warm and carried out in the best "oriental manner." The clever "Edu" Neumann respected Joachim Müncheberg's need for independence without attracting attention, as expressed in the following letter written to *Geschwaderkommodore* Adolf Galland:

Africa, 23/6/1941

Esteemed Herr *Oberstleutnant*!

It was with endless and proud joy that we learned yesterday of our *Geschwader's* great successes and the first-time awarding of the Oak Leaves with Swords to the Herr *Oberstleutnant*. We performed a proper Indian dance, or properly speaking a Negro dance, and I would also like to express my most obedient congratulations on behalf of my *Staffel*. This letter will probably arrive beneath a mountain of mail, but nevertheless I will write at some length, as the brief also has an official purpose.

My fears of going stale in Greece were, thank God, not entirely founded. After about 14 days of rest in Catania I moved to the south Peloponnese.

It is truly desolate in the Peloponnese. Unbelievable heat, much dust, life in tents, and all the while cut off from the outside world. Tactical employment was correspondingly meager, engaging sea targets in the eastern Mediterranean in cooperation with a Stuka-*Gruppe*. This required us

African away game. Left with donkey *Leutnant* Mietusch, 2nd from right Joachim Müncheberg, *Staffelkapitän* of 7./JG 26.

7./JG 26 was temporarily attached to I./JG 27, whose commander was the very popular *Hauptmann* Eduard Neumann.

to fly marine reconnaissance once or twice daily with long-range tanks up to 200 kilometers south of Crete. 2 ½ to 3 hours flying time, of course without any results, as the English fleet is sufficiently tied up in Syria. As well the whole thing was carried out with no air-sea rescue service, and was therefore not very pleasant.

In summer 1941, *I. Gruppe* of JG 27 in Africa was reinforced by 7./JG 26, led by Joachim Müncheberg, seen here after landing.

A happy Müncheberg greets a visiting friend and comrade.

Africa, summer 1941. Rearming one of 7./JG 26's Bf 109s.

Bf 109s take off from a forward airfield in North Africa.

Müncheberg after returning from a sortie over Africa.

A German forward airfield in North Africa.

On 15 July 1941, Müncheberg shot down an enemy fighter that was on the tail of Richard Heller's (1913-1945) aircraft, saving him and his radio operator. It was Müncheberg's 46th victory.

Incidentally, at Molaoi airfield I relieved Major Handrick and his *Gruppe*, which returned to Rumania and is probably now in the East.

I therefore welcomed the Air Commander Africa's call for fighter reinforcements when the Battle of Sollum took on threatening proportions and moved here to the Tobruk area with six aircraft and part of the ground personnel. The remaining pilots were in Catania to collect the last of my machines and could not accompany me. They are now in Greece, and I am trying to convince the corps to let them join me so that I can break in Lindemann and Schleiden here at the front. Actually I should be back already, as the situation has been restored, but by persisting I have hung on a bit longer. I shudder to think of a period of inactivity in Greece or Crete, where we are supposed to go later.

Important decisions will surely be made here in the eastern Mediterranean in the fall, and we fighters will definitely be needed, but until then things look grim. Perhaps I can at least make possible a secondment to Russia. But that is still a long way in the future. For now I am sharing the airfield with Edu Neumann and am even living in the same trailer with him. The heat here is more bearable than in Greece. On the other hand, there are infinitely more flies, and the occasional sandstorms are also unpleasant. So far, however, I have had no problems with the aircraft, even without tropical equipment. As before I am independent and under orders to cooperate tactically with I./JG 27. This has run smoothly, and our welcome has been outstanding as per the rules of the fighter arm. Operationally we have had a little bad luck, and so far only Mietusch and I have been able to shoot down a Hurricane, numbers 10 and 44.

A return to the *Geschwader* still seems to be in the stars, but there is nowhere else that I would want to go. Unfortunately our move has resulted in a breakdown in mail delivery, and we have been sitting here without any mail for three weeks. I therefore know nothing of the *Geschwader* apart from accounts in the *Wehrmacht* communiqué, from which we are able to glean some information. Unfortunately the personal is completely lacking.

Obedient thanks by the way for the transfer of Oblt. Lindemann. I haven't seen him yet because he is always flying behind me. Sitting way out here, one sometimes gets homesick for one's old unit, but feelings must not determine actions at the front. I would only ask, Herr *Oberstleutnant*, that you not forget us. Further, I would ask the Herr *Oberstleutnant* to tell my *Gruppe* how much we appreciate the letters from Hptm. Schöpfel and Oblt. Sprick. There's little time to write here. In conclusion, I again wish Herr *Oberstleutnant* and the *Geschwader* a hearty "Hals und Beinbruch" and, with best wishes to my old comrades, I remain your gratefully devoted

Joachim Müncheberg

In his letter of 23 June 1941, Müncheberg briefly mentioned his and *Leutnant* Mietusch's successes. Here are the facts from the war diary:

Shortly after eight o'clock in the morning South African Hurricanes were

Hauptmann Walter Adolph was killed on 18/9/1941 after 28 victories. On 19 September Müncheberg succeeded him as *Kommandeur* of II./JG 26.

Müncheberg was promoted to *Hauptmann* on 19 September 1941.

encountered. Müncheberg's 44th enemy aircraft fell from the sky about 20 km southeast of Buq Buq at 07:55, while Lt. Mietusch also scored a victory. It is thought that these were aircraft of 2 Squadron SAAF, but they could also have been from 1 Squadron SAAF.

Four days later Müncheberg was successful again. His victim was another Hurricane, but this time a reconnaissance version. The enemy aircraft crashed near Lavyet Ungeila on the morning of 24 June 1941. Its pilot, PO Sowrey of 6 Squadron RAF, was killed.

The days that followed were somewhat quieter for Müncheberg and his men, but on the evening of 15 July 1941 there were fierce combats between Hurricane fighters of 73 and 229 Squadrons and German aircraft in the Tobruk area. The Hurricanes slipped past the Bf 109s and Bf 110s escorting a formation of Stukas and then dove on the slow flying dive-bombers. In a matter of minutes they shot down six of fifteen Ju 87s of II./St.G. 2, plus a Bf 110 of the fighter escort.

Hauptmann Müncheberg joined this action southwest of Ras El Milh, but at first thought he was dealing with a group

Klaus Mietusch (1918-1944), seen here as a *Major* and *Kommandeur* of II./JG 26, succeeded Müncheberg as *Staffelkapitän* of 7./JG 26 on 18 September 1941.

Poster for Luftwaffe quarters: wearers of the highest decorations for bravery. In addition to Mölders, Galland, Oesau, Wick, Bär, Gollob, Priller, other wearers of the Knight's Cross and senior Luftwaffe officers, Joachim Müncheberg may be seen top right wearing the Oak Leaves.

France, 1941: a trio of aces from JG 26, Müncheberg, Schöpfel and Josef "Pips" Priller.

Autumn 1941. In the photo are the fighter aces Galland, Schöpfel, Müncheberg and *Oberst* Huth.

With his beloved dachshund.

of Tomahawks. The effect of his first attack was like swatting a swarm of bees. The twelve Hurricanes scattered in all directions. Müncheberg thought he saw effective strikes on one of the machines, but then he was himself "unpleasantly chased" (original quote) by two of the British fighters. He finally gave his pursuers the slip and then dove towards the Ju 87s and Bf 110s. Müncheberg:

> I soon had my revenge and sent a Curtiss, which went down like a blazing torch, into the sand.

The machine he shot down was more or less right on the tail of a Bf 110, and in doing so he saved the crew of *Oberfeldwebel* Richard Heller (8./ZG 26). What he took to be a "Tomahawk" was in fact a Hurricane of 73 or 229 Squadron, and it crashed in the desert at 18:40. This confirmed victory was number 46 for Joachim Müncheberg. On the British side, PO Lauder and PO Moss failed to return, while the aircraft of Squadron Leader Rosier was badly damaged. This suggests that Müncheberg's first opponent was also shot down.

The following is from a letter written by Müncheberg in those days:

> The P-40 is now appearing in greater numbers down here, consequently our conversion to the "F" slowly appears to be becoming necessary. It is planned for August.
>
> At present our only opportunities for action in the air involve the ships, which are supposed to fight their way into Tobruk and usually have powerful fighter escort.
>
> Otherwise my *Staffel* and I always carry out special operations, for example fighter sweeps over Marsa Matruk (200 to 250 km behind the front) and strafing attacks on columns deep in the enemy rear.
>
> I have little enthusiasm for air defense, with daytime temperatures reaching more than 60 degrees. It's too grueling.
>
> We are always outnumbered by the enemy three to one …

A macabre curiosity: during one of these strafing attacks Müncheberg was hit by rifle fire. His guardian angel was obviously watching over him, for the bullet took off one of the earphones of his headset.

Joachim Müncheberg and his men returned to Sicily at the end of July. During its two-month deployment in North Africa, 7. *Staffel* of *Jagdgeschwader 26* had shot down a total of ten enemy aircraft: five by *Oberleutnant* Müncheberg, two by *Leutnant* Mietusch, and one each by *Feldwebel* Johannsen, *Unteroffizier* Mondry, and *Leutnant* Lindemann, who claimed a bomber.

What could he have been thinking?

8 December 1941: Wevelghem, Belgium. A smiling Müncheberg after recording his 60th victory.

28 December 1941, Coquelles, France. The tail of Müncheberg's Fw 190 A with 61 victory bars.

On 17 March 1942, Müncheberg was awarded the Operational Flying Clasp for Fighter Pilots in Gold.

24 March 1942. The Staffel painter applies victory bar number 65 to the rudder of Müncheberg's Fw 190 A-1 (WNr. 20209).

End of 1941: *Oberst* Joachim-Friedrich Huth (1896-1962), Commander of Fighters 2 in northern France, with officers of the fighter arm. Third from the left in the light-colored jacket is Joachim Müncheberg.

In August 1941 7./JG 26 was transferred back to France.

On 19 September 1941, *Oberleutnant* Müncheberg was promoted to *Hauptmann* and assumed command of *II. Gruppe* of *Jagdgeschwader 26*, replacing the fallen *Hauptmann* Walter Adolph.

His first success in his new role as *Kommandeur* was the downing of a Spitfire on 13 October (victory no. 57). He increased his total to sixty by shooting down two more Spitfires on 8 November and another on 8 December. The reaching of this landmark received mention in the *Wehrmacht* communiqué on 11 December 1941.

Near Le Touquet-Bologne there was a combat with Spitfires of 317 Squadron, during which Müncheberg probably shot down Polish Wing Leader Marian Pisarek (1 Polish Fighter Wing consisting of 303, 316, and 317 Squadrons) at 16:04. It was Müncheberg's 74th confirmed victory.

June 2, 1942, was another "Spitfire day" for Müncheberg, as he shot down two of the RAF fighters in the space of six minutes (between 11:01 and 11:07).

Interestingly, the *Wehrmacht* communiqué of 4 June 1942 only mentioned the round figure of 80 victories.

On 20 June 1942, "Jochen" Müncheberg took his leave as a "Channel fighter pilot" by shooting down two more Spitfires within three minutes (between 15:44 and 15:47).

New challenges were awaiting the young airman on a very different front, challenges that didn't appear to appeal to him.

April 1942. The tail of Müncheberg's Fw 190 A-1 with 67 victory bars. Note the Werknummer 20209, which here is painted in a rather different style.

2 June 1942. Müncheberg describes his 80th victory for Wilhelm Galland. That same day he also scored his 81st victory, six minutes after number 80.

On 15 June 1942 Müncheberg received the German Cross in Gold.

Joachim Müncheberg Profile

Müncheberg as *Kommandeur* of *II. Gruppe* of JG 26.

Hauptmann Joachim Müncheberg with "Wutz" Galland, *Staffelkapitän* of 5./JG 26, and pilots of the *Gruppe*. Wilhelm Ferdinand Galland, brother of Adolf Galland, flew in Müncheberg's *Gruppe* and was killed over Belgium on 2 January 1943 as a *Hauptmann* and *Gruppenkommandeur*. He was awarded the Knight's Cross posthumously on 18 May 1943.

Back from a mission over the Channel. The stress is visible in his face.

Taking advantage of the quiet between sorties.

Issuing orders.

Knight's Cross Profiles — VOLUME 2

Post-mission debriefing.

Müncheberg and Hans Bauer (1897-1993), for 13 years Hitler's personal chief pilot and leader of the "Reich Government" air squadron.

Old master and young up-and-comer in tough competition. The German light athletics championships in the Olympic Stadium in Berlin. Knight's Cross wearer *Hauptmann* Müncheberg (ASV Cologne) practices the decathlon—here the shot put (25/7/1942). The photo is from "Das Sportbild von Schirner," Germany's largest sporting photograph archive.

... after a mission.

Action on the Eastern Front, *Kommodore* of JG 51 – 33 Victories and Three Times Shot Down Himself

On 21 July 1942, Joachim Müncheberg left *II. Gruppe* of *Jagdgeschwader 26* and was sent to the Eastern Front for familiarization with the position of *Geschwaderkommodore*. He was less than enthusiastic about the fact that he had been selected as a future commander of a *Geschwader*. Part of what set him apart was his enormous strength of will and his fierce thirst for action, paired with calm consideration. In truth, these characteristics made him ideally suited to command a *Geschwader* with more than 150 aircraft. Instead, however, Müncheberg felt somewhat thwarted, restricted by the bureaucracy that came with this command position. In a letter he wrote:

> What am I supposed to do with a *Geschwader*? I have more than enough paperwork to do now!
> It means nothing more than an increase in that and a reduction in my ability to lead in the air. I would much prefer to remain in command of a *Gruppe* …
> Of necessity one must have the required inner maturity and experience before filling a more senior position.

With 83 victories, Müncheberg was one of the Luftwaffe's most successful aces in the west and, like many pilots on the Western Front, he initially held the opinion that the air war in the east was sort of child's play by comparison. His initial over-confidence had its price, however. Müncheberg very quickly paid the price for underestimating the Russian airmen. In his first two weeks on the Eastern Front he was shot down twice.

Despite this, his victory total continued to rise rapidly. He made his debut on the Eastern Front on 3 August 1942, and within just five minutes, from 10:32 to 10:36, he sent two Pe-2 bombers crashing to the ground. He scored his next victory the following day at almost exactly the same time. At 10:38 he downed an "iron Ivan," an Ilyushin Il-2 armored close-support aircraft. The next day, 5 August 1942, a LaGG-3 fighter aircraft fell prey to Müncheberg's accurate fire.

Snapshots between two missions.

Shop talk among Channel experts. Müncheberg and Egon Meyer of JG 2 "Richthofen."

In the evening hours of 4 September 1942, Müncheberg shot down another Pe-2 which crashed south of Zubtsovo. It was victory number 99. On 5 August 1942, after the *Kommodore* of JG 51 *"Mölders"* (Oak Leaves wearer Karl-Gottfried Nordmann, 1915-1982) was wounded and put out of action, Müncheberg took over command of the *Geschwader* on an acting basis.

That same evening he would reach and surpass the "hundred mark," scoring a double in the Kubinka area. At 17:53 he shot down an American-made P-39 Airacobra for his one-hundredth victory, and four minutes later destroyed a second. The evening

175

Müncheberg's decorations included the Italian pilot's badge, awarded to him for his actions in the Mediterranean theater.

Generalfeldmarschall Hugo Sperrle (1885-1953), commander-in-chief of *Luftflotte* 3, visits II./JG 26 on the Channel Coast.

Russia, late summer 1942. On 22 July Joachim Müncheberg (2nd from left) joined the *Geschwader* headquarters of JG 51 for familiarization in the post of *Kommodore*. He is seen here in conversation with *Kommodore* Karl-Gottfried Nordmann (5th from left). The *Gruppenkommandeur* of III./JG 51, Hptm. Karl-Heinz Schnell (4th from left), was awarded the Knight's Cross on 1/8/1941. Schnell scored a total of 72 victories.

Hauptmann Leppla of JG 51 with a head dressing after being wounded. Müncheberg is on the left. This is one of the few photos taken while he was with JG 51.

missions flown in those days were extremely productive for the ambitious airman. Victories 99 to 103 (an Il-2 on 09/09/42) were all scored between 17:00 and 18:00. In the days and weeks that followed, the *Staffel* painter had plenty to do. The paint on the tail of Müncheberg's machine scarcely had time to dry in September, when 23 victory bars had to be added. His last success on the Eastern Front was dated 27 September. Early in the morning, at 07:03, he shot down a LaGG-3. On 9 September 1942, after 103 victories, Müncheberg became the 19th member of the armed services and 13th fighter pilot to be awarded the Knight's Cross with Swords.

On 22 July 1942, after Karl-Gottfried Nordmann was wounded, Müncheberg assumed command of *Jagdgeschwader* 51 "Mölders" in the east.

Following his 103rd victory, on 9 September 1942 Müncheberg became the 19th member of the German armed forces and 13th fighter pilot to receive the Knight's Cross with Swords.

"Always ready to leap into action," a visit with *Hauptmann* Müncheberg. This was the title of an article about Müncheberg in the Luftwaffe magazine "Der Adler."

Success over Africa as *Kommodore* of JG 77

On 1 October 1942 Müncheberg was named *Kommodore* of *Jagdgeschwader 77*, which was supposed to move from the southern sector of the Eastern Front to North Africa. He succeeded *Major* Gordon Gollob (1912-1987, third recipient of the Knight's Cross with Swords and Diamonds), who had led the unit since 16/5/1942. The Luftwaffe command was planning to relieve the now-exhausted fighter units deployed in North Africa. The first to leave was III./JG 53, which left North Africa and flew to Sicily.

On 27 October, *Jagdgeschwader 77* moved to the African continent, to Ain el Gazala in Libya. Among the *Staffel* commanders in *Hauptmann* Heinz Bär's *I. Gruppe* were two of the leading aces in the *Geschwader*, indeed, the entire German fighter arm. *Hauptmann* Friedrich Geißhardt (1919-1943) had 91 victories to his credit and was the 101st recipient of the Oak Leaves, while *Oberleutnant* Siegfried Freytag (1919-2003) had 70 victories and wore the Knight's Cross. The *Gruppe's* pilots also included *Leutnant* Heinz-Edgar Berres (1920-1943), who was *Gruppe* adjutant, and would be awarded the Knight's Cross posthumously on 19 September 1943 after 52 victories; and *Leutnant* Armin Köhler (1912-1999), who when the war ended would command *III. Gruppe* of JG 77, and who was awarded the Knight's Cross after 40 victories.

As the *Geschwader* arrived in Africa without ground personnel, it was initially forced to rely on *I. Gruppe* of *Jagdgeschwader 27* for logistical support in operations against the English advance.

On 28 October, *III. Gruppe* came under the command of *Hauptmann* Kurt "Kuddel" Ubben (1911-1944), 80th recipient of the Oak Leaves. Ubben had 92 victories to his credit. His *Staffel* commanders were the fighter aces *Hauptmann* Wolf-Dieter Huy (1917-2003, 83rd recipient of the Oak Leaves, victor in 39 air combats, and an anti-shipping specialist), *Oberleutnant* Erich Omert (1918-1944, wearer of the Knight's Cross and another "*Experte*" with 53 victories), and *Oberleutnant* Helmut Gödert, who had 25 victories to his credit.

The *Geschwaderstab* under Müncheberg, equipped with new Bf 109 G-2s, was expected to arrive in Africa one day later. Müncheberg had "desert experience" from his days as *Staffelkapitän* of 7./JG 26, and his victory total now stood at 116. The initial optimism

Hauptmann **Müncheberg shortly after receiving the Oak Leaves and Swords.**

soon faded, however, for he and his men soon found themselves facing a hopeless situation. Then, at the end of November, Müncheberg was promoted to *Major* for bravery in the face of the enemy, his third preferential promotion.

The newly-promoted *Major* found himself again facing western opponents who were made of sterner stuff than their Soviet comrades.

At that time the command positions in the *Geschwaderstab* were manned as follows:

Kommodore:
  Major Joachim Müncheberg
Geschwader Adjutant:
  Oberleutnant Theo Lindemann
Geschwader Operations Officer:
  Oberleutnant Helmut Meckel
Geschwader Technical Officer:
  Oberleutnant Horst Huck
Special Duties Officer:
  Hauptmann Erich Woitke
Special Duties Officer:*
  Hauptmann Erwin Bascillia

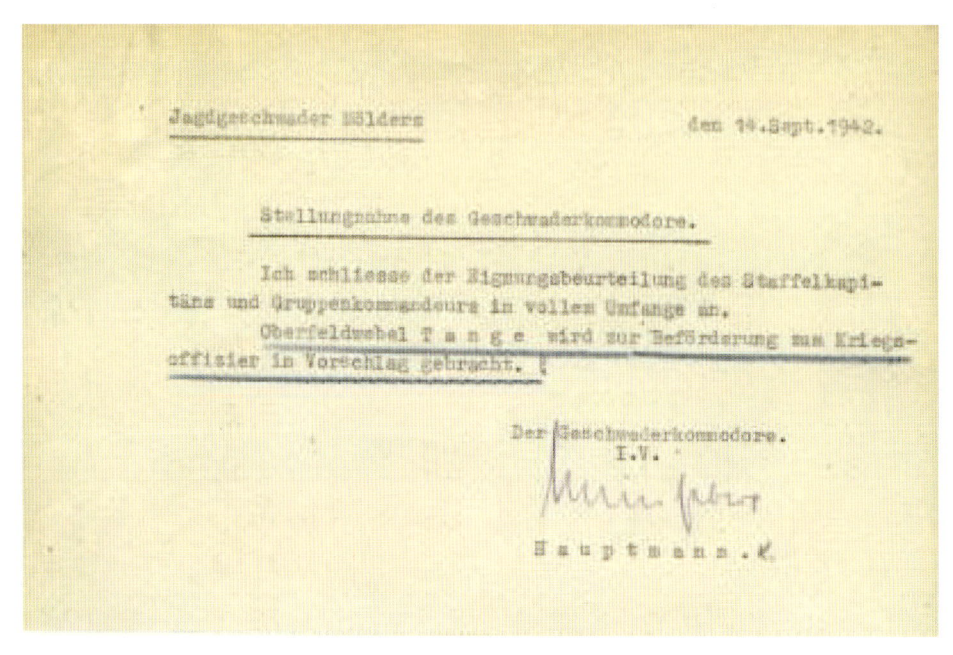

14 September 1942: one of the unpopular administrative tasks of a *Kommodore*, as he described in a letter. This is his endorsement of officer training for *Oberfeldwebel* Otto Tange (1915-1943, Knight's Cross on 19/3/1942) of II./JG 51.

*The two so-called "special duties officers" were transferred to JG 77 to "prove themselves at the front." Hptm. Woitke had been commander of II./JG 52, while in the summer of 1941 Hptm. Bascillia had commanded the German-Rumanian fighter units responsible for defending the Ploesti oil fields.

Despite facing an opponent with a marked numerical superiority, Müncheberg shot down 19 more Anglo-American aircraft.

On the morning of 9 November 1942, a Monday, elements of JG 77 were in the air guarding roads between Sidi Barrani and Sollum. *Hauptmann* Bär shot down a P-40 for his 126th victory. *Oberleutnant* Geißhardt, *Staffelkapitän* of 3./JG 77, and *Oberfeldwebel* Schumann of 1./JG 77 were also successful. Then, in the afternoon the staff flight took off to conduct a fighter sweep and protect roads in the Buq-Buq area, subsequently engaging seven Spitfires. *Major* Müncheberg shot down a Spitfire V at 15:07. The pilot was Flight Sergeant Blades of 92 Squadron RAF. It was his 117th victory. Müncheberg claimed another, but it was not confirmed.

At that time the *Stab*, plus *I.* and *III Gruppe* of JG 77, were stationed in Bir-el-Arca, where Müncheberg assembled his pilots for a briefing on 9 November. The following is an excerpt from Armin Köhler's diary:

Major Müncheberg held a briefing. The Africa Corps is in pretty rough shape. He read out an order from Göring to the fighter pilots in Africa. It was less than gratifying, and one can only wonder about how wrongly the situation is assessed from above. The fighters are, so to speak, responsible for Rommel having to retreat. The fighter pilots in Africa have a different opinion. All of them!

As we are receiving no supplies, when we have no aircraft left we are supposed to pick up a rifle and fight to the end with the Africa Corps, and if necessary go down with it. Müncheberg said that we will probably never see Europe again."

On 24 November 1942, German and Italian commanders met in Arco Philaenorum to discuss the subsequent

Major Gordon Gollob (1912-1987), third recipient of the Diamonds, commanded JG 77 from 16 May 1942 until he was relieved by Müncheberg.

Müncheberg was promoted to *Major* on 30 November 1942.

Back in Africa, Joachim Müncheberg as *Kommodore* of JG 77.

prosecution of the war. There was a brief conversation between *Major* Müncheberg, the *Kommodore* of JG 77, and *Generalfeldmarschall* Kesselring, the commander-in-chief in the Mediterranean. The latter remarked of Müncheberg that he was the right man in the right place at the right time.

Early on the morning of 27 November 1942, eight Bf 109s of JG 77 took off. Among them were three machines of the *Geschwaderstab*. At 07:32, during an engagement with about a dozen Spitfires (1 Squadron SAAF), Major Müncheberg shot down the aircraft of Lt. Marshall. It was his 118th victory.

December 10, 1942, a Thursday, saw an increase in activity by Allied reconnaissance aircraft, suggesting that an attack on the Marsa-el-Bregha position

Hans-Joachim Marseille (1919-1942), 4th recipient of the Diamonds, was also awarded the Italian Gold Medal of Bravery on 6 August 1942. He and Müncheberg were the only foreigners to receive the decoration.

Heinz Bär in Tunisia.

Major Heinz Bär, *Kommandeur* of III./JG 77, in conversation with *Kommodore* Müncheberg. 2nd from right is Armin Köhler, and next to him is Ofw. Herbert Boennle (1920-1943) of JG 54.

Generalfeldmarschall Erwin Rommel (1891-1944) visits JG 77. Müncheberg (left) listens as one of his pilots reports. Rommel (center) puts on his life vest and then listens to Müncheberg's report.

Hauptmann Wolf-Dieter Huy in front of his Bf 109 G-2/trop. "White 1" (WNr. 13633). His personal successes are marked on the aircraft's tail. The aircraft behind it also has an impressive victory tally.

was imminent. Allied fighter-bombers were also active, and in the afternoon a scramble from Arco Philaenorum airfield by eight aircraft led by Müncheberg was able to prevent the worst. The Messerschmitts engaged a formation of Spitfires and Curtiss, and pursued the enemy far out over the sea.

At 15:05 *Major* Müncheberg recorded his 119th victory, downing a P-40 of the 66th Fighter Squadron, 57th Fighter Group twelve kilometers northwest of Agheila. The *Kommodore* did not escape the combat untouched, however. He was forced to land his Bf 109 G-2 (WNr. 10 725) at Arco Philaenorum with hits in the engine. The emergency landing resulted in a crash which resulted in damage assessed at 35%. Luckily Müncheberg escaped injury.

On the afternoon of 14 December 1942, eight Messerschmitts of *III. Gruppe* scrambled and then assembled under Müncheberg's command to pursue eight American-flown Curtiss P-40s of the 57th Fighter Group. The latter were attacking ground targets beneath a top cover of other P-40s. During the period from 15:08 to 1525 Müncheberg scored victories 120 and 121.

As 1943 began, the British Eighth Army was nearing the port city of Tripoli in Libya. The German and Italian forces of the Africa Corps withdrew into southern Tunisia to establish a new defense line in the fortified Mareth Position. For the first time since the retreat from El Alamein, the Axis powers began to regain a foothold. They received air support from *Jagdgeschwader 77*, whose three *Gruppen* were now all in North Africa under Müncheberg's command.

Early on the morning of 15 December 1942, a dozen Kittyhawks of 250 Squadron RAF attacked vehicle columns on the road from Arco to El Agheila.

In the ensuing combat *Feldwebel* Siegfried Ott of 1./JG 77 was shot down and captured west of El Agheila. Shortly before noon eleven Curtiss, this time from 260 Squadron RAF, engaged roughly the same number of Messerschmitts. Müncheberg, who was leading two flights (*Schwärme*) from III./JG 77, forced a P-40F to make a belly landing on the coast near Ras el Aaali at 11:58.

North Africa. Rommel's personal transport, a Heinkel He 111 H6 (VG + ES).

A German airfield in Tunisia.

The *Experten* of JG 77

Heinz Bär (1913-1957), *Kommandeur* of I./JG 77 in Africa. Knight's Cross on 2/7/1941, Oak Leaves on 14/8/1941, Swords on 16/2/1942. Final rank *Oberstleutnant*.

Wolf-Dieter Huy (1917-2003), KCC on 5/7/1941, 83rd Oak Leaves on 17/3/1942. Final rank *Hauptmann*.

Karl "Kuddel" Ubben (1911-1944), KCC on 4/9/1941. 80th Oak Leaves on 20/3/1942. Final rank *Major*.

Friedrich Geißhardt (1919-1943), KCC on 30/8/1941. 101st Oak Leaves on 23/6/1942. Final rank *Hauptmann*.

Heinz-Edgar Berres (1920-1943), KCC on 19/9/1943. Final rank *Hauptmann*.

Armin Köhler (1912-1999), KCC on 7/2/1945. Final rank *Major*.

… and the *Kommodore* Joachim Müncheberg.

1943 – On the Retreat in Africa

While on the ground the British continued to build up their forces in front of the Buerat Position, in the air the Desert Air Force effectively committed its units in low-level attacks against ground targets. The aircraft were in the air early, and at 08:00 *Oberleutnant* Laube and *Oberfeldwebel* Niederhagen (both of 3./JG 77) shot down two P-40s.

Not long afterwards a large group of bombers was reported heading towards Bir Dufan, and *I. Gruppe* was immediately scrambled. Several aircraft of the *Geschwaderstab* under *Major* Müncheberg (with *Hauptmann* Woitke as his wingman) joined up. Northeast of the airfield the German fighters intercepted 18 twin-engined Baltimores of 21 Squadron SAAF. Müncheberg brought down one of the South African bombers at 08:45.

Despite fierce sandstorms, 14 January 1943 proved a busy day for the *Geschwader*. *I. Gruppe*'s war diary recorded about 240 enemy aircraft in the area around Bir Dufan. The air raid warning was sounded there shortly after 11:00. Roughly 18 Boston bombers with a powerful escort of P-40s were approaching the airfield. Fierce dogfights broke out moments later, in which *Major* Müncheberg shot down three Kittyhawks between 11:17 and 11:23. He now had 126 victories to his credit. Late in the afternoon on 18 January 1943 Joachim Müncheberg, along with seven aircraft, engaged American P-40s, one of which

Leutnant Armin Köhler's Bf 109 G-2/trop "White 3."

One of the last photographs of Müncheberg.

he was able to shoot down. His victim went down five kilometers southeast of Tarhuna at 16:40.

The German retreat seemed to be picking up speed. Tripoli was abandoned and the port facilities destroyed. Stab/JG 77 left Castell Benito after a brief stay and moved to Zuara, a forward airfield 150 km west of Tripoli on the Via Balbia. At about noon *Major* Müncheberg took off, accompanied only by his wing man, *Oberfeldwebel* Niederhagen (I./JG 77), to intercept a group of 21 P-40 fighter-

On 14 March 1943 in Gabes, *Hauptmann* Müncheberg decorated Oblt. Günther Rübell (left) of 5./JG 51 and Ofw. Otto Schulze of 6./JG 51 with the Knight's Cross for their success in Africa. On the right is *Hauptmann* Hartmann Grasser, *Kommandeur* of II./JG 51. At that time II./JG 51 was attached to JG 77 under *Kommodore* Müncheberg.

bombers attacking vehicle columns flooding back along the Via Balbia. Between 12:55 and 13:05 Müncheberg reduced the attacking force by two Kittyhawks.

A few days after his latest double success Joachim Müncheberg, now with 129 victories to his credit, went on home leave—his last. First, however, he went to Berlin, where a meeting was scheduled with the *General der Jagdflieger* Adolf Galland. Müncheberg then spent three weeks in Zürs, in Tyrol.

At the beginning of March 1943, the *Geschwader* began receiving new aircraft. The *Stab* and *I. Gruppe* were first to receive the new Bf 109 G-6/trop variant. The proven basic design had been modified again. In addition to heavier armament, the G-6 also had a new FuG 16 VHF radio.

Major Müncheberg returned from leave on 7 March 1943 and resumed command of the *Geschwader*. Of course, he immediately began flying the new G-6. *Stab*/JG 77 was by then based in La Fauconnerie. The Allies were steadily reducing the Tunisian bridgehead. A day earlier a German attack against the Eighth Army from the Mareth Position had failed with heavy losses in tanks. On

Ju 52s over Tunisia in the spring of 1943.

One of his passions, accordion playing.

10 March 1943 "Jochen" Müncheberg claimed two victories: victory number 130 came at 16:33, 131 at 16:48. On Friday, the 13 March 1943, he scored his 132nd and 133rd victories.

March 22, 1943, was a Monday. On both sides land operations were hampered by heavy rain, but in the air there were fierce combats, and Müncheberg shot down a Curtiss P-40 flown by Flt.Sgt. Maloney of 250 Squadron at 14:27. Twelve Kittyhawks from that squadron were providing fighter escort for another twelve P-40s of 112 Squadron attacking Axis vehicle columns in the El Hamma area. *Jagdgeschwader 77* lost four pilots that day. Even worse was to come one day later.

Fatal Crash

At about 09:30 on 23 March 1943, a Tuesday, *Major* Müncheberg and his wing man, *Leutnant* Strasen, took off from La Fauconnerie airfield and headed for the Mareth area to see if their was anything there to shoot down. It was his 500th combat mission. Near Sened the pair ran into about 15 Spitfires of the American 52nd Fighter Group. Though clearly outnumbered, the Germans immediately accepted combat, and *Kommodore* Müncheberg soon found himself surrounded by enemy fighters. The wild dogfight moved steadily closer to the ground, with the German pilots fully exploiting their experience. Müncheberg singled out Captain Theodore Sweetland, the American formation leader, and—probably coming from below and behind—attacked and set his machine on fire. Sweetland went down in flames in a steep turn. It was Müncheberg's 135th and final victory. Then his airman's fate was fulfilled.

Joachim Müncheberg had almost distanced himself from his opponents southwest of Maknassy when the wings of his Bf 109 G-6 (WNr. 16381) came off in a tight defensive turn and he crashed to his death. According to *Leutnant* Strasen, his machine went down after colliding with pieces of Captain Sweetland's Spitfire. Captain Hugh L. Williamson, who was later shot down by Strasen, said that Sweetland, in his burning Spitfire, had intentionally rammed Müncheberg's 109. Neither pilot had been able to closely follow the course of the fateful combat. All three aircraft crashed near Kilometer Stone 82 on the Gabes to Gafsa road. *Leutnant* Strasen managed to give the Spitfire formation the slip and flew to Fatnassa, where the *Geschwader*'s I. *Gruppe* was based.

Leutnant Karl-Heinz Rentrop, a former member of JG 77, remembered:

> One day *Leutnant* Strasen of the *Geschwaderstab* landed at our airfield and climbed from his

On 23 March 1943, Joachim Müncheberg crashed to his death in Tunisia after scoring his 135th victory. He was buried in El Aonnia, and was later reinterred in the military cemetery at Les Massem, near Tunis.

El-Aouina-*Leutnant* Gerhard Strasen carries the decorations pillow during the funeral.

Messerschmitt stony-faced. To *Hauptmann* Bär he simply said: "*Herr Hauptmann*, Jochen is dead!" A *Storch* immediately took off for the crash site. There they discovered the wreckage of Müncheberg's 109 — he had crashed still within shooting distance behind the Spitfire.

Major Müncheberg was thrown from the aircraft and died of his injuries on the way to hospital.

Gerhard Strasen described Müncheberg's final combat from a wing man's point of view in a latter to the author on 8 March 2001:

On 23 March 1943 Müncheberg and I flew a mission. We were flying above the clouds when, through a hole in the clouds, we saw two Spitfire beneath us. I informed Müncheberg, who immediately attacked the aircraft flying below us. Our speed was very great, and he got too close to the aircraft, which exploded under his fire and took him down with it.

The loss of the *Kommodore* was an especially heavy blow to the *Geschwader*. In just five months with the *Geschwader*, *Major* Müncheberg, considered one of the most capable unit commanders in the entire fighter arm, had earned the respect and affection of every man in the unit. It was largely due to his energetic and skillful command that JG 77 survived the retreat from El Alamein to the Tunisian border as a fighting unit, not only maintaining its cohesion, but also achieving considerable success in the battle against the numerically superior Allied air forces. With 19 victories during this period, Müncheberg also played a significant part in this success. With the death of Joachim Müncheberg on 23 March 1943, the entire Luftwaffe lost not just one of its most successful fighter pilots, but also one of its acknowledged best unit leaders, whose human and professional qualities were valued equally.

Müncheberg was initially buried in a soldier's grave near El Aouina, then his body was moved to the military cemetery

On 1 April 1943 *Oberstleutnant* Johannes Steinhoff succeeded Müncheberg as *Kommodore* of JG 77.

A propaganda service photo released after Müncheberg's death ...

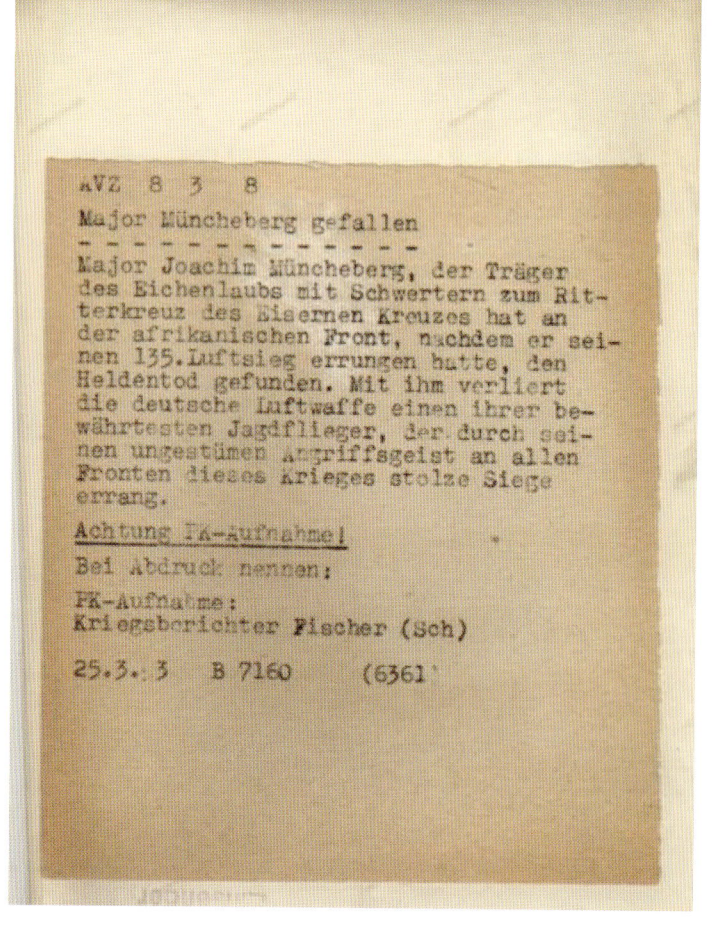

... and the text on the reverse side.

Joachim Müncheberg's List of Victories

No.	Date	Time	Type	Unit	Location	Remarks
1	07/11/1939	13:43	Blenheim I	Stab III./JG 26	SW of Opladen	(L1325) 57 Squadron RAF, flown by P/O HR Bewley, POW
2	11/05/1940	17:45	Curtiss Hawk H 75A	Stab III./JG 26	NNW of Antwerp	GC I/4 Armée de l'Air
3	14/05/1940	18:45	Hurricane	Stab III./JG 26	E of Ath	504 Squadron RAF
4	19/05/1940	13:00	Hurricane	Stab III./JG 26	near Overijse	(L1645) 3 Squadron RAF flown by Sgt. JLC Williams, fatally wounded
5	29/05/1940	18:10	Spitfire	Stab III./JG 26	W of Dunkirk	64, 229 or 610 Squadron RAF
6	31/05/1940	15:35	Westland Lysander	Stab III./JG 26	Furnes-Dunkirk	--
7	31/05/1940	15:40	Hurricane	Stab III./JG 26	SW of Dunkirk	213 or 264 Squadron RAF
8	31/05/1940	15:45	Hurricane	Stab III./JG 26	NE of Dunkirk	213 or 264 Squadron RAF
9	31/05/1940	20:10	Spitfire	Stab III./JG 26	Channel – Dunkirk	609 Squadron RAF
10	28/07/1940	15:15	Hurricane	Stab III./JG 26	15 km NE of Dover	257 Squadron RAF
11	08/08/1940	12:55	Spitfire	Stab III./JG 26	NE of Margate	65 Squadron RAF
12	14/08/1940	13:29	Hurricane	Stab III./JG 26	Folkestone-Dover	32 or 615 Squadron RAF
13	15/08/1940	16:01	Spitfire	Stab III./JG 26	Calais-Folkestone	64 Squadron RAF
14	24/08/1940	12:22	Hurricane	7./JG 26	Ashford	151 Squadron RAF
15	31/08/1940	10:00	Hurricane	7./JG 26	NW of Braintree	56 Squadron RAF
16	01/09/1940	14:52	Hurricane	7./JG 26	W of Goodhurst	79 or 85 Squadron RAF
17	06/09/1940	10:28	Hurricane	7./JG 26	Dungeness	303 Squadron RAF
18	07/09/1940	18:45	Spitfire	7./JG 26	SE of London	603 Squadron RAF
19	11/09/1940	19:25	Spitfire	7./JG 26	E of Ashford	66 or 92 Squadron RAF
20	14/09/1940	17:05	Spitfire	7./JG 26	S of Maidstone	222 Squadron RAF
21	17/10/1940	14:55	Bloch 151	7./JG 26	S of Faversham	--
22	25/10/1940	14:40	Spitfire	7./JG 26	Marden	92 Squadron RAF
23	14/11/1940	15:32	Spitfire	7./JG 26	Channel, SE of Dover	66 or 74 Squadron RAF
24	12/02/1941	16:41	Hurricane	7./JG 26	SW of Siggiwi, over Malta	261 Squadron RAF
25	16/02/1941	10:38	Hurricane	7./JG 26	SW of Malta	261 Squadron RAF, damaged
26	16/02/1941	10:45	Hurricane	7./JG 26	E of Venezia, Malta	(V7731) 261 Squadron RAF, flown by F/L JAF MacLachlan, baled out wounded
27	25/02/1941	16:45	Hurricane	7./JG 26	E of St. Paul's Bay, Malta	261 Squadron RAF
28	26/02/1941	14:06	Hurricane	7./JG 26	S of Krendi, Malta	(V7671) 261 Squadron RAF, flown by F/O FF Taylor, fatally wounded
29	26/02/1941	14:10	Hurricane	7./JG 26	10 km S of Malta	261 Squadron RAF
30	02/03/1941	10:45	Hurricane	7./JG 26	2 km W of Marsa Scirocco, Malta	806 Squadron FAA
31	05/03/1941	17:32	Hurricane	7./JG 26	S of Hal Far, Malta	261 Squadron RAF
32	15/03/1941	07:50	Wellington	7./JG 26	10 km NW of Gozo	(W5644) of the Reserve Flight, Stradishall, RAF
33	28/03/1941	17:32	Hurricane	7./JG 26	10 km S of Gozo	261 Squadron RAF
34	06/04/1941	12:05	Avia BH-33E Fury	7./JG 26	NE of Podgorica	Ind. Fighter Esk, 81st (Bomber) Grupa, JKRV, flown by Porucnik Milenko Milivojevic, fatally wounded
--	06/04/1941	--	Avia BH-33E Fury	7./JG 26	Podgorica	Ind. Fighter Esk, 81st (Bomber) Grupa, JKRV – destroyed on ground, not recognized as victory
--	06/04/1941	--	Breguet XIX	7./JG 26	Podgorica	destroyed on ground, not recognized as victory
35	11/04/1941	11:31	Hurricane	7./JG 26	SE of Malta	261 Squadron RAF
36	11/04/1941	11:53	Hurricane	7./JG 26	SE of St. Paul's Bay, Malta	(V7116) 261 Squadron RAF, flown by P/O PA Mortimer, crash-landed
37	23/04/1941	18:07	Hurricane II	7./JG 26	SE of Hal Far	(L5807) 261 Squadron RAF, flown by F/O FM Auger, fatally wounded
--	27/04/1941	--	Short Sunderland	7./JG 26	Kalafrana Bay, Malta	(L5807) 228 Squadron RAF, destroyed on ground, not recognized as victory
38	29/04/1941	18:47	Hurricane	7./JG 26	St. Paul's Bay, Malta	261 Squadron RAF
39	01/05/1941	07:53	Hurricane II	7./JG 26	SE of St. Paul's Bay, Malta	(Z2900) 261 Squadron RAF, flown by P/O HA Innes, wounded
40	01/05/1940	07:54	Hurricane II	7./JG 26	SW of Ta Venezia	(Z3061) 261 Squadron RAF, flown by Sgt. BC Walmsley, wounded
41	01/05/1941	17:15	Hurricane	7./JG 26	SW of Luqa airfield	261 Squadron RAF
42	06/05/1941	12:22	Hurricane II	7./JG 26	NE of St. Paul's Bay	(Z3060) 261 Squadron RAF, flown by P/O CK Gray, baled out wounded
43	06/05/1941	12:26	Hurricane II	7./JG 26	1 km SW of Hal Far	(Z3059) 261 Squadron RAF, flown by Sgt. RA Branson, baled out
--	25/05/1941	15:00	Hurricane	7./JG 26	Takali	249 Squadron RAF, destroyed on ground, not recognized as victory
--	25/05/1941	15:00	Hurricane	7./JG 26	Takali	249 Squadron RAF, destroyed on ground, not recognized as victory
44	20/06/1941	07:55	Hurricane	7./JG 26	20 km E of Buqu-Buqu	1 or 2 Squadron SAAF
45	24/06/1941	08:00	Hurricane	7./JG 26	Lavyet Ungila	6 Squadron RAF, flown by P/O JAF Sowrey
46	15/07/1941	18:40	Hurricane	7./JG 26	SW of Ras el Milh	73 or 229 Squadron RAF
47	29/07/1941	17:48	P-40 Tomahawk	7./JG 26	50 km E of Bardia	2 Squadron SAAF
48	29/07/1941	17:52	P-40 Tomahawk	7./JG 26	40 km E of Bardia	2 Squadron SAAF
49	28/08/1941	19:30	Spitfire	7./JG 26	2 km N of Gravelines	--

Knight's Cross Profiles

No.	Date	Time	Type	Unit	Location	Remarks
50	29/08/1941	08:40	Spitfire	7./JG 26	10 km NE of Dunkirk	--
51	04/09/1941	17:26	Spitfire	7./JG 26	Bollezeelen	--
52	04/09/1941	17:29	Spitfire	7./JG 26	Zeggers	--
53	07/09/1941	17:22	Spitfire	7./JG 26	NW of Montreuil	71 Squadron RAF
54	16/09/1941	19:40	Spitfire	7./JG 26	E of Boulogne	306 or 315 Squadron RAF
55	18/09/1941	16:06	Hurricane	7./JG 26	Yvetot	607 Squadron RAF
56	18/09/1941	16:15	Spitfire	7./JG 26	St. Helene	452 Squadron RAF
57	13/10/1941	14:33	Spitfire	Stab II./JG 26	Samer	--
58	08/11/1941	13:07	Spitfire	Stab II./JG 26	Loon-Plage	412 Squadron RCAF, Digby Wing
59	08/11/1941	13:15	Spitfire	Stab II./JG 26	NE of Dunkirk	412 Squadron RCAF, Digby Wing
60	08/12/1941	14:17	Spitfire	Stab II./JG 26	W of Boulogne	--
61	16/12/1941	16:01	Spitfire	Stab II./JG 26	NW of Dunkirk	411 Squadron RCAF
62	16/12/1941	16:04	Spitfire	Stab II./JG 26	N of Gravelines	411 Squadron RCAF
63	13/03/1942	16:17	Spitfire	Stab II./JG 26	Wivre Effroy	124 Squadron RAF
64	24/03/1942	16:30	Spitfire	Stab II./JG 26	NW of Rue-Cambron	412 Squadron RCAF
65	24/03/1942	16:35	Spitfire	Stab II./JG 26	Cambron	412 Squadron RCAF
66	4/4/1942	11:46	Spitfire	Stab II./JG 26	W of Calais	--
67	10/4/1942	17:50	Spitfire	Stab II./JG 26	NW of Etaples	340 Squadron RAF
68	25/4/1942	16:40	Spitfire	Stab II./JG 26	SW of Crécy	--
69	25/4/1942	16:43	Spitfire	Stab II./JG 26	SW of Ruen	--
70	26/04/1942	18:05	Spitfire	Stab II./JG 26	WNW Calais	485 Squadron RNZAF
71	26/04/1942	18:06	Spitfire	Stab II./JG 26	10 km W of Cap Gris Nez	485 Squadron RNZAF
72	27/04/1942	14:47	Spitfire	Stab II./JG 26	NW of Dunkirk	the Tangmere Wing or 340 Squadron RAF
73	27/04/1942	16:06	Spitfire	Stab II./JG 26	N of Mardyck	303 Squadron RAF
74	29/04/1942	16:04	Spitfire	Stab II./JG 26	Le Touquet	the Northolt Wing or 303 Squadron RAF
75	30/04/1942	19:36	Spitfire	Stab II./JG 26	W of the Somme Estuary	222 Squadron RAF
76	01/05/1942	19:31	Spitfire	Stab II./JG 26	SW of Calais	122 or 222 Squadron RAF
--	01/05/1942	19:40	Spitfire	Stab II./JG 26	5 km N of Calais	victory not confirmed, no witnesses
77	06/05/1942	18:53	Spitfire	Stab II./JG 26	NW of Cap Gris Nez	303 Squadron RAF
--	09/05/1942	13:43	Spitfire	Stab II./JG 26	15 km S of Gravelines	118 or 501 Squadron RAF, victory not confirmed, no witnesses
--	09/05/1942	13:44	Spitfire	Stab II./JG 26	15 km S of Gravelines	118 or 501 Squadron RAF, victory not confirmed, no witnesses
--	17/05/1942	17:35	Spitfire	Stab II./JG 26	Guines-St. Omer	victory not confirmed, no witnesses
78	31/05/1942	19:37	Spitfire	Stab II./JG 26	S of Crécy Forest	485 Squadron RNZAF
79	31/05/1942	19:41	Spitfire	Stab II./JG 26	Quend Plage des Pins	302 Squadron RAF
80	02/06/1941	11:01	Spitfire	Stab II./JG 26	SW of Abbeville	403 Squadron RCAF
81	02/06/1941	11:07	Spitfire	Stab II./JG 26	15 km W of Étaples	403 Squadron RCAF
82	20/06/1942	15:44	Spitfire	Stab II./JG 26	S of Ardres	118 or 501 Squadron RAF
83	20/06/1942	15:47	Spitfire	Stab II./JG 26	E of Boulogne	118 or 501 Squadron RAF
84	03/08/1942	10:32	Pe-2	Stab/JG 51	Grid square 47 591	--
85	03/08/1942	10:36	Pe-2	Stab/JG 51	Grid square 47 514	--
86	04/08/1942	10:38	Il-2	Stab/JG 51	6 km NE Zubtsov	--
87	05/08/1942	18:48	LaGG-3	Stab/JG 51	Grid square 47 880	--
88	09/08/1942	14:30	MiG-3	Stab/JG 51	Grid square 47 844	--
89	10/08/1942	18:40	Yak-1	Stab/JG 51	Grid square 47 563	--
90	22/08/1942	10:25	Il-2	Stab/JG 51	Grid square 47 761	--
91	24/08/1942	06:20	Il-2	Stab/JG 51	Grid square 47 754	--
92	24/08/1942	06:21	Il-2	Stab/JG 51	Grid square 47 791	--
93	25/08/1942	17:11	Pe-2	Stab/JG 51	Grid square 47 381	--
94	02/09/1942	08:23	LaGG-3	Stab/JG 51	SW of Karmanovo	--
95	02/09/1942	10:52	Il-2	Stab/JG 51	SW of Gzhatsk	--
96	02/09/1942	10:55	Il-2	Stab/JG 51	SSW of Gzhatsk	--
97	02/09/1942	10:55	Il-2	Stab/JG 51	SSW of Gzhatsk	--
98	03/09/1942	14:32	Il-2	Stab/JG 51	Grid square 46 192	--
99	04/09/1942	17:35	Pe-2	Stab/JG 51	S of Zubtsovo	--
100	05/09/1942	17:53	P-39	Stab/JG 51	Kubinka	--
101	05/09/1942	17:57	P-39	Stab/JG 51	Grid square 66 380	--
102	09/09/1942	17:08	Il-2	Stab/JG 51	Grid square 47 733	--
103	09/09/1942	17:12	Il-2	Stab/JG 51	Grid square 47 762	--
104	10/09/1942	07:09	Pe-2	Stab/JG 51	Grid square 47 843	--
105	10/09/1942	07:13	Il-2	Stab/JG 51	Grid square 47 764	--
106	10/09/1942	10:35	LaGG-3	Stab/JG 51	Grid square 47 811	--
107	14/09/1942	07:35	Il-2	Stab/JG 51	Grid square 47 762	--
108	14/09/1942	17:01	Il-2	Stab/JG 51	Grid square 47 594	--
109	14/09/1942	17:13	Il-2	Stab/JG 51	Grid square 47 591	--
110	14/09/1942	17:17	Pe-2	Stab/JG 51	Grid square 47 732	--
111	22/09/1942	09:25	MiG-3	Stab/JG 51	Grid square 47 612	--
112	22/09/1942	09:31	R-5	Stab/JG 51	Grid square 47 611	--
113	26/09/1942	12:23	LaGG-3	Stab/JG 51	Grid square 47 522	--
114	26/09/1942	16:08	LaGG-3	Stab/JG 51	Grid square 47 572	--
115	27/09/1942	06:59	LaGG-3	Stab/JG 51	Grid square 47 592	--
116	27/09/1942	07:03	LaGG-3	Stab/JG 51	Grid square 47 612	--

No.	Date	Time	Type	Unit	Location	Remarks
117	09/11/1942	15:07	Spitfire V	Stab/JG 77	E of Buq Buq	92 Squadron RAF flown by F/Sgt. Bates
--	09/11/1942	--	Spitfire	Stab/JG 77	--	No witnesses, victory not Confirmed
118	27/11/1942	07:32	Spitfire	Stab/JG 77	--	1 Squadron SAAF, flown by Lt. Marshall
119	10/12/1942	15:05	P-40 F	Stab/JG 77	12 km NW of Agheila	66th Fighter Squadron, 57th Fighter Group USAAF
120	14/12/1942	15:08	P-40 F	Stab/JG 77	SW of Agheila	57th Fighter Group USAAF
121	14/12/1942	15:25	P-40 F	Stab/JG 77	SW of Agheila	57th Fighter Group USAAF
122	15/12/1942	10:58	P-40	Stab/JG 77	Ras el Aali	--
123	13/01/1943	08:45	Baltimore	Stab/JG 77	--	--
124	14/01/1943	11:17	P-40	Stab/JG 77	--	--
125	14/01/1943	11:21	P-40	Stab/JG 77	--	--
126	14/01/1943	11:23	P-40	Stab/JG 77	--	--
127	18/01/1943	16:40	P-40	Stab/JG 77	--	--
128	22/01/1943	12:55	P-40	Stab/JG 77	--	--
129	22/01/1943	13:05	P-40	Stab/JG 77	--	--
130	10/03/1943	16:33	P-40	Stab/JG 77	--	--
131	10/03/1943	16:48	P-40	Stab/JG 77	--	--
132	13/03/1943	15:04	P-40	Stab/JG 77	--	--
133	13/03/1943	17:51	P-40	Stab/JG 77	--	--
134	22/03/1943	14:27	P-40	Stab/JG 77	--	--
135	25/03/1943	09:50	Spitfire	Stab/JG 77	SW Al Miknasi, Algeria	--

On 23 March 1943, Joachim Müncheberg crashed to his death after scoring his 135th victory. He was buried in El Aonnia and was later reinterred in the military cemetery in Les Massem, near Tunis.

The plaque bearing Joachim Müncheberg's name.

Joachim Müncheberg's final resting place.

in Les Nassen, near Tunis, where more than 500 other members of the Luftwaffe are buried.

As it took time to name a successor, the *Kommodore* of JG 53, *Oberstleutnant* von Maltzahn, also assumed temporary command of JG 77. *Oberstleutnant* Johannes Steinhoff, Müncheberg's successor as *Kommodore*, arrived on 1 April 1943.

Steinhoff, who then had 156 victories to his credit, led the *Geschwader* under the most difficult conditions in Tunisia, and then in Italy against an enemy far superior in materiel. On 28 July 1944 he became the 82nd member of the armed forces to be decorated with the Oak Leaves and Swords.

With the death of Joachim Müncheberg on 23 March 1943, the Luftwaffe lost a successful fighter pilot whose human and professional qualities were tremendously high. In 500 combat missions he had shot down 135 enemy aircraft, including 33 in the east, 19 over Malta, one in Yugoslavia, and 24 in North Africa. He was thus one of the small circle of German fighter pilots to achieve more than 100 victories against western opposition. Always a disciplined and chivalrous soldier and an exemplary, modest, and correct man, Müncheberg met his fate in the Tunisian theater of war.

Turning to philosophy, his motto always was "Understand that life teaches you that there is more to honor than honors."

On 25 March 1943 the *Wehrmacht* communiqué reported:

Major Müncheberg, decorated with the Knight's Cross of the Iron Cross with Oak Leaves and Swords, died a hero's death after his 135th victory.

Barely two months after *Major* Müncheberg's death, Army Group Africa surrendered.

A bust of Müncheberg in the former Luftwaffe museum in Uetersen.

Joachim Müncheberg, unforgotten.

Sources:

Joachim Müncheberg's sister Eva Hoffstätter-Müncheberg (+)
Gerhard Strasen (Müncheberg's wingman and good friend from his civilian days)
Wolfgang Westerwelle Archive, Ralf Schumann Archive
J. Müncheberg's personnel file in the Bundesarchiv
AERO Magazine
Josef Priller: *JG 26 – Geschichte eines Jagdgeschwaders*, Motorbuch
Ring/Shores: *Luftkampf Zwischen Sand und Sonne*, Motorbuch
Shores/Ring/Hess: *Tunisien 42/43 – Luftkämpfe über Fels und Wüste*, Motorbuch
Aders/Held: *Jagdgeschwader 51 Mölders*, Motorbuch
Held/Obermaier: *Die deutsche Luftwaffe im Afrika-Feldzug*, Motorbuch
Edward H. Sims: *Jagdflieger – Die großen Gegner von einst*, Motorbuch
Karl-Heinz Faltermeier: *Joachim Müncheberg und seine Flugzeuge 1941/42*, Luftfahrt International 12/81.
Jochen Prien: *Geschichte des Jagdgeschwaders 77 – Teil 3*, Struve

Photos:

Ralf Schumann Archive
Wolfgang Westerwelle Archive
André Hüsken (Hamburg)

Text and Research:

Wolfgang Westerwelle, Ralf Schumann

Acknowledgments:

The authors are especially grateful to Manfred Franzke of UNITEC Media Sales and Distribution who, by publishing this book, made it accessible to a wide readership. I am also grateful to Eva Hoffstätter-Müncheberg (+) and Gerhard Strasen for their kind support during my research.

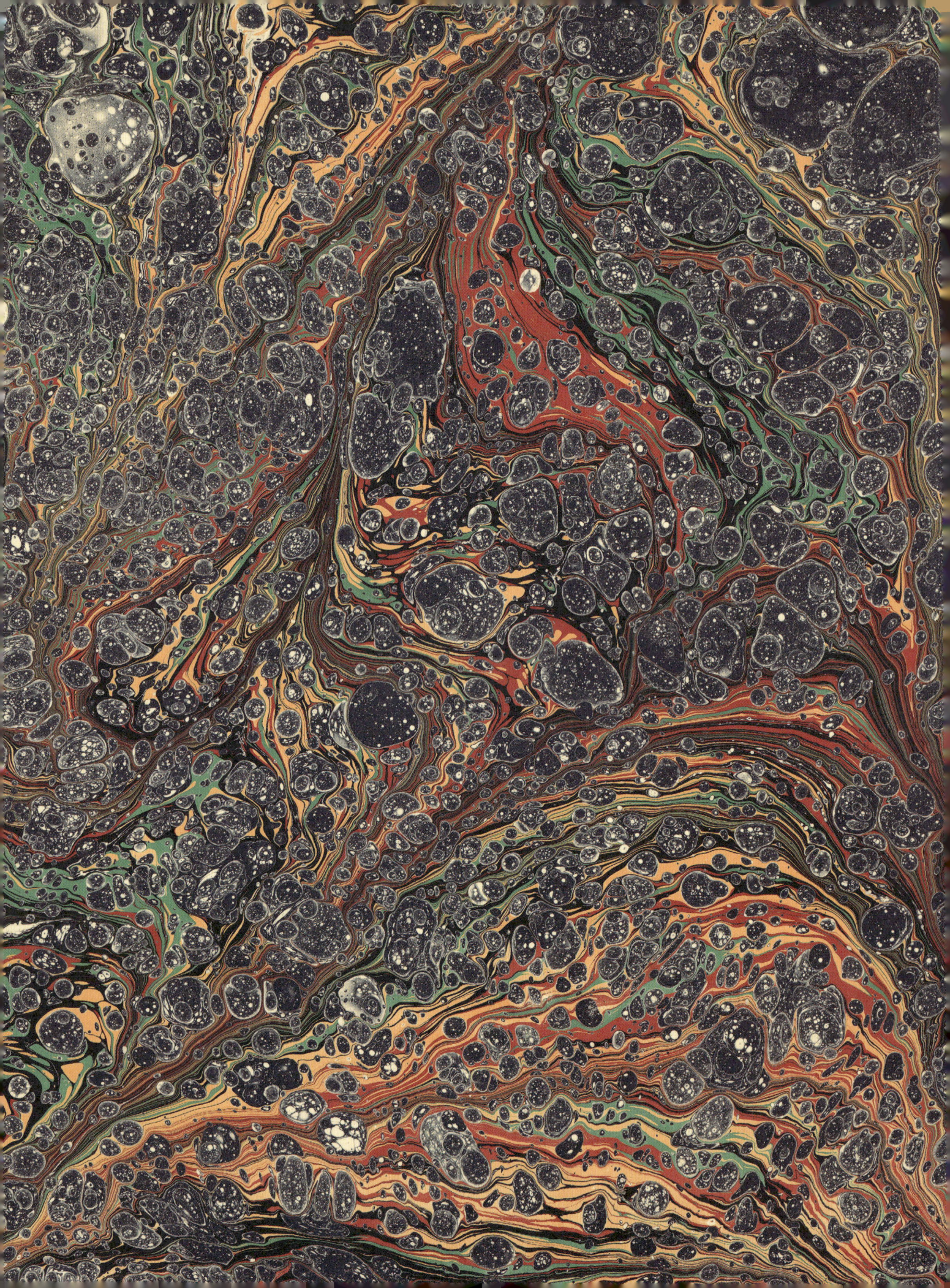